TUHAMI

TUHAMI
Portrait of a Moroccan

Vincent Crapanzano

The University of Chicago Press

Chicago and London

The University of Chicago Press, Chicago 60637
The University of Chicago Press, Ltd., London

©1980 by The University of Chicago
All rights reserved. Published 1980
Paperback edition 1985
Printed in the United States of America
94 93 92 91 90 89   6 5 4

Library of Congress Cataloging in Publication Data

Crapanzano, Vincent, 1939–
    Tuhami, portrait of a Moroccan.

    Bibliography: p.
    Includes index.
    1. Ethnology—Morocco. 2. Tuhami. 3. Ethnology—
Fieldwork. 4. Morocco—Social life and customs.
5. Morocco—Biography. 6. Psychoanalysis. I. Title.
GN649.M65C7   301.29′64   79-24550
ISBN 0-226-11870-3 (cloth)   0-226-11871-1 (paper)

To Jane

The myth does not exist that is not the

ever-renewed revelation of a reality

which so imbues a being that he makes

his behavior conform to it. Short of

this, it slowly hardens into a story

which will become cold one day.

MAURICE LEENHARDT (1979)

Contents

Preface

Tuhami is an experiment. Whether it is a successful one or not I cannot say. Ever since my first experience of field work—it was with Haitians in New York City, for a course in anthropological field methods with Margaret Mead—I have been deeply concerned with the anthropologist's impress on the material he collects and his presentation of it. Anthropologists have been inclined to proclaim neutrality and even invisibility in their field work; certainly they have tended to efface themselves in their descriptive ethnographies. I have come to believe that in doing so they have acted in what Jean-Paul Sartre (1956) would call bad faith and have presented an inaccurate picture of ethnography and what it can reveal. I do not mean to imply insincerity or prevarication on the part of the individual anthropologist; I want only to call attention to a culturally constituted bias, a scotoma or blind spot, within the anthropological gaze.

By eliminating himself from the ethnographic encounter, the anthropologist can deny the essential dynamics of the encounter and end up producing a static picture of the people he has studied and their ways. It is this *picture,* frozen within the ethnographic text, that becomes the "culture" of the people. The ethnographic encounter, like any encounter between individuals or, for that matter, with oneself in moments of self-reflection, is always a complex negotiation in which the parties to the encounter acquiesce to a certain reality. This "reality" belongs (if it is in fact possible to speak of the possession of a reality removed from any particular social or endopsychic encounter) to none of the parties to the encounter. It is—and this is most important— usually presumed to be the reality of one's counterpart to which one has acquiesced, to expedite the matter on hand. This presumption, which is rarely articulated as such in most ongoing social transactions, gives one the comforting illusion of knowing one's counterpart and his reality. Expressed within a pragmatic mode ("to expedite the matter on hand"), it permits a certain disengagement from the reality of the transaction. The disengagement helps to insulate the parties to the encounter from the repercussions of failure. It permits, too, a superior stance in the inevitable jockeying for power that occurs within such negotiations.

In the ethnographic encounter, where the matter at hand is the knowledge of the Other and his reality, there is a very strong compulsion to attribute the negotiated reality to one's informant. There are, to be sure, all sorts of analytic strategies that have been devised to distinguish between what is specific to an encounter and what is typical, general, or even universal. Such strategies, which include multiple and repetitive questioning in different contexts, the use of several modes of elicitation, the search for pattern, consistency, and redundancy, confirmation in the research of others, the evaluation of informants, and, ultimately, self-reflection and evaluation, must be regarded with a certain skepticism, for they may—and often do—serve as rationalizations for the objectification of the negotiated reality and its attribution to the Other. They frequently presuppose a degree of lucidity that is impossible for any participant within the encounter. The anthropologist has no more privileged access to lucidity than did the impassioned heroes of Racinian tragedy.

I am not making a plea for subjective anthropology. I do not wish to deny the anthropological enterprise, as some critics have tried to do (Hymes 1974), or to proclaim a *new* anthropology. I wish rather to call attention to an essential feature of the ethnographic encounter and its effect upon the anthropologist's productions. I believe that such a critical understanding is necessary for a realistic evaluation of the anthropological endeavor and the ethical and political role of its practitioners—a role that is so often masked behind one ideology or another. (I am aware of the fact that my argument, too, is the product of an ideology, which, from within, I would characterize as self-reflective, involuted, inevitably circular, ironic, and not without a certain iconoclasm.) My point here is that, as anthropologists, we have a responsibility to the people we study, if not to our readers, to recognize the ethical and political implications of our discipline. Every interpretive strategy, including those implicit within description itself, involves choice and falls, thereby, into the domain of ethics and politics.

Tuhami is a complicated work. It is a life history of a Moroccan tilemaker who was married to a she-demon, a *jinniyya,* named 'A'isha Qandisha. It is also an attempt to make sense of what Tuhami the tilemaker related to me the anthropologist and to come to some understanding of how he articulated his world and situated himself within it. It raises the question of his freedom and the constraints, both within him and without, on that freedom. Above all—and I write with uneasiness and a certain regret—"Tuhami" both as text and as a fellow human being enables me to raise the problematic of the life history and the ethnographic encounter. Tuhami becomes, thereby, a figure within an imposed allegory that in a very real sense bypasses him. My own obtrusive presence in his life not only enables Tuhami to tell his story; it also permits me the luxury of entering that allegory in the name of a science that is unknown to him. Through that science, through anthropology, my position with respect to Tuhami is rationalized. Knowingly, I have made that choice.

Much has been written in recent years about the role of symbols in social and ritual life, but little has been written about the role such symbols play in the individual's life or its articulation. Anthropologists like Clifford Geertz, Victor Turner, and, above all, Nancy Munn have all suggested that cultural and ritual symbols affect the way in which the individual experiences his world; but they have not, to my knowledge, looked in detail to the individual to substantiate their suggestions. There is, of course, no way that we can know, except perhaps through an empathetic leap, how the symbols are appreciated within the conscious life of another individual. We *can* learn how an individual uses the symbols in his portrayal of reality. This distinction is important. We can know, in other words, the rhetoric of symbols, but we cannot know, except hypothetically, how symbols are experienced. I do not try, in this book, to give a view of Moroccan culture from within. The attempt to discover what a culture looks like from personal-historical documents has always struck me as an act of great naïveté. Rather, I look at the way in which Tuhami makes use of the particular idiom at his disposal to articulate his own experience, including his personal history within *our* negotiations of reality. With less perspective perhaps, certainly with greater resistance, I look at the use I make of my own idiom within our negotiations.

Tuhami is, as I have said, an experiment designed to shock the anthropologist and the reader of anthropology from the complacency with which they have succumbed to the determinants of their respective endeavors: the writing and reading of ethnography. (The doing of anthropology has usually been considered with considerably more anguish and puzzlement—an anguish and puzzlement that are themselves becoming conventions of the discipline.) It is for this reason, as I explain in the Introduction, that I have tried not to follow a conventional form in writing about my encounter with Tuhami.

The study as it *now* stands consists of five parts framed by an Introduction and an Epilogue. The Introduction presents Tuhami and raises the question of personal history and the genres into which it is cast. Parts One, Three, and Five are records of Tuhami's recitations. They include my questions and my explanations of references that may be obscure to the reader unfamiliar with Moroccan culture. I have also included certain interpretations of what Tuhami was saying or doing that I believe will render the recitations less opaque to the Western reader. They reveal, at least, my own bias. Part Two, in which I attempt to understand the recitations from within the framework of Moroccan culture, is necessarily static and so belies that process of continual negotiation from which it is generated. It says something about the nature of Moroccan social relations, the meaning of the pilgrimage, self-alienation, and the individual's use of cultural and ritual symbols. It discusses the nature of Tuhami's recitations and offers, at least implicitly, a theory of recitation. Part Four is a more personal meditation on the nature of field work, the use of a field assistant, and my encounter with Tuhami. It is concerned with the knowledge of other individuals. The Epilogue speaks for itself.

I have placed Parts Two and Four, the principal theoretical sections, within the recitation to stress the extent to which ethnological theory is embedded with the specific ethnographic encounter. Theorizing in anthropology, particularly in the United States but elsewhere as well, has been characterized by a certain "nervousness": an ad hoc if not hip-shooting approach to "problem areas," whose consequent isolation is masked by a perseverated concern for context; a flighty borrowing of "models" from other "disciplines"; a mistrust of—or a stubborn, simplistic faith in—such large theoretical edifices as Marxism, psychoanalysis, or Parsonian sociology; a debunking of past masters, who remain, nevertheless, primary, reverential reference points; a self-righteous squabbling over *the* correct method, interpretive strategy, analytic tactic, or theoretical instrument; a jealous guarding of the anthropological dominion, frequently accompanied by imperial forays into other dominions; and an anxious affirmation of anthropology as a science. I exaggerate the negative. My conceit is psychological. My aim is to emphasize the degree to which theory itself is a response to the encounter and to the burden that encounter imposes on the psyche of the investigator. Theory serves also to formulate the encounter and its burdens or, perhaps more accurately, to valorize the idiom through which the encounter and its burdens are formulated.

In this work I make use of several different theoretical positions that are not, from the strictest point of view, fully consistent or even compatible. Sartre's emphasis on lucidity and Freud's on blindness are cases in point. They, like Simmel, the symbolic anthropologists, Lacan, and certain contemporary literary critics provide the theoretical space in which my encounter with Tuhami, with Morrocco more generally, took place. I believe, indeed I have to believe, that there is a certain consistency, an elegance even, in my theoretical vision. I use specific theoretical approaches here rhetorically—to illuminate the space of encounter and what I believe, from my essentially skewed position, transpired within it. My reference, then, to theorists and theories resembles rather more the references that literary critics, in their interpretation of a specific text, make to other authors than it resembles the references that anthropologists and other social scientists make in their development of theory. For the critic the text has a primacy that data—the social scientist's text—do not have. To speak too simply, data for the social scientist are frequently sacrificed to theory; for the critic, theory is sacrificed to the text. In *Tuhami* I struggle to sacrifice neither the one nor the other and thereby risk a double sacrifice.

For the sake of readability I have used as few Arabic expressions as possible. They should, nevertheless, all be immediately recognizable to the student of Arabic. Again for the sake of readability, I have, whenever I could do so without distorting Tuhami's meaning or tone, eliminated vocatives, such as *A Sidi* ("Oh, Sir"), and conventional invocations to God and the saints, such as *l-hemdullah* ("Thank God") and *'ensha' llah* ("God willing," which is required in any reference to the future). To translate these gives to a distinctly colloquial language a stilted and archaic quality.

I have used a minimum of footnotes and have included in the Bibliography only works directly referred to or quoted in the text. I am, as will be evident to the reader, greatly indebted to the writings of Jean-Paul Sartre, particularly to his study of Jean Genet (1964), which served to counter a psychoanalytic bias in my perception and thinking. I do not advocate and have never advocated, even in my earlier studies of the Hamadsha, a reductive psychoanalytic position. Reductionism is the antithesis of good anthropology and humane psychoanalysis. Anthropology should, I believe, lead us to question, not to confirm, our own presumptions.

•   •   •

The research on which this study is based was supported by grants from the National Institutes of Mental Health (MH-13776-01), the Institute of Intercultural Research, and Princeton University. Joanne Magdoff, Judith Goldstein, Carl Thun, James Clifford, Paul Zweig, and Burton Pike have all been kind enough to read the manuscript and offer helpful suggestions. I have also received helpful suggestions from the participants in my seminar at Harvard entitled Self and Other in Anthropological Research and from the participants in the Colloquium on Psychoanalytic Methods and Questions in Anthropological Fieldwork at the 1978 Annual Meeting of the American Psychoanalytic Association in New York. The colloquium, which lasted through two intense afternoons, was devoted to a discussion of "Tuhami." I should like to thank my field assistant, who prefers the anonymity of "Lhacen." Without him this study would not have been possible. I should also like to thank

Dorothy Reisman, who typed and retyped the several versions of the manuscript. I am most grateful to my wife, Jane Kramer, who has helped me with exquisite patience through all the phases of the study. She knew and admired Tuhami as I did. I wish, finally, to thank my daughter Wicky, who from the ages of five through eight has had to live through all the moodiness and impatience that accompanies the writing of a book.

Introduction

— Pasha Hammu's son had four wives. Each wife was big and fat. I ran errands for the pasha's son and took his women to the baths after he had slept with them. I watched over them on feast days.

— How did you begin to work for the pasha's son?

— He came to my quarter and saw me playing. He asked whose son I was. I answered, "Fatima's." He called for her and asked if I were her son. My mother answered, "No. Why do you ask?" He said that he wanted me to work for him, that she could come to see me whenever she wanted. She told him that she would have to ask her husband. The pasha's son said, "I'll take him right now. His father can come over and discuss it with me." He gave me three candies. Finally my mother agreed. "I'll come to see him in the morning," she said.

As soon as we got to his house, I was sent to the baths. When I got back, I was given new clothes: a *jallaba*, a *tarboosh* from Marrakech, and a silver dagger. I was given other clothes too. I thought to myself that, even if my parents didn't want me to work here, I would. The next morning my mother came to see me. She asked what I wanted to do. I said it was up to her, and she told me to stay.

— Were you glad to stay?

— Yes. The pasha's son had only one daughter. He was rich. He had four wives! But he saw them maybe once a week. He was always with other women.

— How were the women?

— They were always nice to me. They gave me treats, clothes, even meals. One day they asked me a question: "What does our husband do when he goes out?" I told them I couldn't answer. They began to kiss and fondle me, to feed me candies. Finally I told them that their husband was visiting other houses. "Our life is over," one of the wives moaned.

The pasha's son was a fox. He understood right away what had happened. He called me into his room and took me by the ear. "What did you tell my wives?" he asked. The women pleaded with him from behind the door not to beat me. "We were walking one day," they said, "and saw you enter a house." That is how I got away. He let me go. He told me to get out. I left the room, and a few minutes later he called me back in. "The next time one of these women asks you where I've been," he said, "tell her to take a walk with you. The moment she leaves the house, slam the door in her face." I said that was shameful. "There is no shame in such matters," he answered.

Then the pasha's son and I left the house. He ordered me to knock at a certain door. A woman came to the door and asked who was there. I said it was the pasha's son. The woman was afraid. She was breathing heavily. The pasha's son entered. The women he slept with came out. We all ate together. Then the pasha's son took me to the market to buy clothes: shoes, socks, and other clothes. "We'll go to see your mother," he said afterward. We drank tea and ate a little with my mother and then went back to his house. He did all this to make up to me because he had pulled my ear.

A week later my father died. It was the Prophet's birthday. The pasha's son said that if he found anyone working in his district that day he would fine him. He said that if a rich man had died everyone would have gone to his funeral. "Now," he said, "everyone will have to go to the funeral of a poor man." He meant my father.

•   •   •

Tuhami was an illiterate Moroccan Arab tilemaker, and I am beginning my portrait of him with this fragment from his personal history because it raises the question of his, of any, personal history.* I have been unable to integrate it into the narrative text of his life. I am unable to omit it. It resists integration because it probably never took place. It sounds more like a fragment from some *Arabian Nights* than the recollection of a

---

*An adaptation of part of this Introduction appeared under the title *The Life History in Anthropological Field Work* (Crapanzano 1977b).

contemporary Moroccan worker. It precludes omission because it speaks a truth that can only be called autobiographical. It was Tuhami who first taught me to distinguish between the reality of personal history and the truth of autobiography. The former rests on the presumption of a correspondence between a text, or structure of words, and a body of human actions; the latter resides within the text itself without regard to any external criteria save, perhaps, the I of the narrator (Frye 1976). Their equivalence is, I believe, a Western presumption.

I have retained this fragment, too, I admit, because I find it nearly impossible to part with any of Tuhami's stories. I am certain that the reader, on coming to know Tuhami, will understand my feelings, perhaps even better than I do. From the beginning, Tuhami fascinated me as a fellow man whose gentleness I came to appreciate, whose integrity, whose character, whose intention, or *niyya,* I came to admire, and whose suffering, however oddly expressed, I came somehow to understand.

Tuhami was exceptional. He was considered an outsider, an outcast even, by the people around him. He lived alone in a dank, windowless hovel near the kiln where he worked, and his privacy was entirely respected. He was often humored, and with his acquaintances—they were many—he had a sort of joking relationship. But he was also treated with awe and a certain deference; he was not considered dangerous, like the outcasts believed to be sorcerers or said to have the evil eye. Tuhami was married to a capricious, vindictive she-demon, a camel-footed *jinniyya,* a spirit, named 'A'isha Qandisha, who kept a firm control on his amorous life. His arrangement with 'A'isha was rare but by no means unique (Crapanzano 1973). (Other Moroccan men were said to be 'A'isha's husbands; they were all peculiar in their way—loners, sexual inadequates, physical misfits, eccentrics, or men who for one social reason or another were unable to marry.) Lalla 'A'isha, that is, "Lady" 'A'isha, as Tuhami always called her, was a jealous lover and demanded absolute secrecy in her marital affairs. In her other relationships with human beings—she could strike them or take possession of them—she made no demands of secrecy. Indeed, these other relationships were public and had to be mediated through the curing ceremonies, the trance-dances, of such exorcistic brotherhoods as the Jilala, the Gnawa, and especially the Hamadsha. Unlike her husbands, her victims in these relationships led more or less normal family lives.

I was directed to Tuhami by a number of Moroccans who had learned of my interest not only in the Hamadsha, the brotherhood I had come to Morocco to study, but in 'A'isha Qandisha. They said nothing directly to me about Tuhami's demonic marriage—they could not; but they told me that Tuhami knew a lot about 'A'isha's ways and the ways of the Hamadsha. He was not, however, a Hamdushi, a member of the brotherhood, and that intrigued me. He could not participate in their rituals or undergo their cure. As in the tale of the pasha's son, he was an outsider. I have sometimes thought that my Moroccan friends arranged for our meeting because they saw a similarity in our position.

• • •

Tuhami's tale of the pasha's son, like many of the other tales he told me, stands midway between history and fairytale. The fairytale, Suzanne Langer has observed, is "irresponsible":

> It is frankly imaginary, and its purpose is to gratify wishes, "as a dream doth flatter." Its heroes and heroines, though of delightfully high station, wealth, beauty, etc., are simply individuals; "a certain prince," "a lovely princess." The end of the story is always satisfying, though by no means always moral; the hero's heroism may be slyness or luck quite as readily as integrity or valor. The theme is generally the triumph of an unfortunate one—an enchanted maiden, a youngest son, a poor Cinderella, an alleged fool—over his or her superiors, whether these be kings, bad fairies, strong animals (e.g., Red Riding Hood's wolf), stepmothers, or elder brothers. In short, the fairytale is a form of "wishful thinking," and the Freudian analysis of it fully explains why it is perennially attractive, yet never believed by adults even in the telling. [Langer 1957, p. 175]

History can be conceived, somewhat too simply to be sure, as the opposite of the fairytale. It is concerned with reality, even reality that doth not flatter, with men and women of all stations, wealth, and beauty, and it ends as it did *in fact* end, however satisfying or unsatisfying that ending may be. It is objective, morally neutral, and certainly not a product of "wishful thinking." It is to be believed. The contrast here depends on the absolute distinction between the *imaginary* and the *real* that has dominated Western thought (cf. Lacan 1966). The imaginary—the product of unconstrained desire at its limit—is relegated to a status inferior to that of the real, which parades under the standard of truth. The problem of what is or is not real is left to the philosopher. To Everyman, the real is both distinct from the imaginary and at one with truth.

This contrast between the fairytale and history suggests, however, that historical texts themselves resemble rather more often the fairytale than history. The historical text, like all texts, including those concerned with personal history, may be conceived as a verbal objectification of the tension between "reality" (resistance, in phenomenological terms) and desire. Both "reality" and desire are structured, as is the text itself, by the idiom at the disposal of its author. Tuhami's tale objectifies, then, the tension between a desire we have yet to understand and a reality we can know no more of than the psychoanalyst can know of the reality his patients purport to describe. His tale carries implicitly, if not explicitly, the Moroccan values, interpretational vectors, patterns of association, ontological presuppositions, spatiotemporal orientations, and etymological horizons that are embedded in his idiom (Crapanzano 1977a). It reflects, for example, the traditional Moroccan social hierarchy, patterns of authority, and attitudes toward paternal and maternal figures, men and women, sexual relations, siblings, and masters and servants. In the permitted "blend" of the imaginary and the real, in the infusion of desire into reality, it reflects conventional and generic constraints.

any tale will reveal tale's cult constructs

The subject of Tuhami's tale is ontologically different from the subject of those tales with which we in the West are familiar. Generic differences are not simply formal differences. They are cultural constructs and reflect those most fundamental assumptions about the nature of reality, including the nature of the person and the nature of language, that are considered, if they are considered at all, self-evident by the members of any particular cultural tradition. The recognition of such differences, of the possibility of another more or less successful way of constituting reality, is always threatening; it may produce a sort of epistemological vertigo and demand a position of extreme cultural relativism (Crapanzano 1977d). Wittingly or unwittingly, however, the anthropologist or his reader often causes the differences to disappear in the act of translation. Such translation may render bizarre, exotic, or downright irrational what would have been ordinary in its own context. The ethnography comes to represent a sort of allegorical anti-world, similar to the anti-worlds of the insane and the child. The ethnographic encounter is lost in timeless description; the anguished search for comprehension in the theoretical explanation; the particular in the general; the character in the stereotype.

It was in reaction to this sort of allegory that I set out to write my portrait of Tuhami. Like the autobiography and the biography, the life history and the case history are literary genres, and, as such, they shape a particular preselected range of data into a meaningful totality (cf. Rosaldo 1976). They reflect not only the more superficial concerns of a particular historical epoch or a particular cultural tradition but also, and more importantly, the more fundamental attitudes toward and evaluations of the person, of time, nature, the supernatural, and interpersonal relations. The Freudian case history, which provided a model for subsequent psychiatric and anthropological case histories, reflects, for example, the distinctive Romantic genre of the *Bildungsgeschichte*. Such a genre, as M. H. Abrams has observed in his *Natural Supernaturalism* (1971), translates "the painful process of Christian conversion into a painful process of self-formation, crisis, and self-recognition, which culminates in a stage of self-coherence, self-awareness, and assured power that is its own reward."

The case history, like the biography, presents a view of the subject from the perspective of an outsider; it bears the impress of a narrator who may even permit himself the luxury of "objectively" analyzing and evaluating his subject. The life history, like the autobiography, presents the subject from his own perspective. It differs from autobiography in that it is an immediate response to a demand posed by an Other and carries within it the expectations of that Other. It is, as it were, doubly edited: during the encounter itself and during the literary (re)-encounter. Not only do the specific questions posed by the Other reflect certain generic expectations within his own culture, but the very question of life history itself may be an alien construct for the subject and cause in him an alienating *prise de conscience*. The frequent elimination of the Other, at least in the form of a narrative I, renders the life history timeless and static. Ironically, this elimination of the I in the name of objectivity would totally preclude both clinical and cultural evaluation were it not that the voice of the Other sounds through its own self-expurgated text (Crapanzano 1978).

Although the life history and the autobiography can be distinguished in terms of the demand of the Other, such a distinction is in the final analysis superficial. The life history and the autobiography, all writings for that matter, are essentially self-constitutive; they are moments, fixed in time by the word, in the dialectical process of self-creation. They require, as such, the mediation of an Other. "The individual," writes the American sociologist George Herbert Mead (1964), "experiences himself as such, not directly, but only indirectly, from the particular standpoints of other individual members of the same social group or from the generalized standpoint of the social group as a whole to which he belongs." The Other includes not simply the concrete individual who stands before one but all that he stands for symbolically. At the most abstract level, he is the transcendental locus of meaning; he is also typified by social roles, conventionalized perceptions, culturally determined styles, and a whole array of idiosyncratic associations that may be less than conscious. He is, to use the language of psychoanalysis, the object of transference.

It is precisely this more abstract Other whom the psychoanalyst in his analysis of the transference relationship attempts to locate in parental figures and other figures of primary significance in his patient's life, often without realizing that he, like his patient, is performing a metaphorical act. The Other may very well be the empty space of desire that can be described only metaphorically. This, at least, is how I read the Oedipus myth and Freud's interpretation of it. (So, too, can Aristophanes' myth of primordial man/woman be read in Plato's *Symposium.*) Through an act of substitution, the son's desire for the mother is replaced by his desire for other women symbolic of his mother. Where the strict Freudians go wrong, I believe, is where they regard the mother (or even her imago) as the *real* object of desire rather than as itself a metaphorical substitute. They take the myth too concretely in its enactment and miss the essential structure of human desire, which precludes such nonsymbolic determination.

The life history is a product of its author's desire for recognition by this essentially complex Other. It is not simply informative; it is evocative as well. Its evaluation requires an understanding of the relationship between the author and his Other, the inevitable interlocutor whom he is addressing. To evaluate the significance of Tuhami's tale of the pasha's son, for example, it would be necessary to understand his desire for recognition both by me, the concrete but symbolically typified individual whom he is directly addressing, and by a more abstract, less transient Other who is for the moment more or less embodied in me and from whom he derives that sense of continuity that we call personal identity. His tale as a whole and each segment of it are a demand, too, for recognition by the pasha's son or whomever he represents, by the son's women or whomever they represent, by Tuhami's mother, his father, and the pasha's son's only child, a daughter.

Tuhami's tale, it seems to me, expresses the desire to be recognized as exceptional. (This desire is itself exceptional in a society that lays less stress on the exceptional than on the conforming.) But there is never enough evidence within the text to determine to whom exactly it is metaphorically addressed. Indeed, I have often thought that it is the indeterminate identity of the interlocutor that produces the reader's fascination with any text. It is as though the reader, in his "suspended disbelief," relentlessly pursues the identity of this interlocutor whom he himself is made to embody. His momentary identifications with characters, made so much of in some literary critical theories, impress me as pauses—surrenders, really, to symbolic substitutes—in the pursuit of the indeterminate, the mysterious, the singular interlocutor.

I have attempted to resist conventional forms in this portrait, but it will not, I think, be altogether unfamiliar to the reader. The reader will recognize too, especially in my questions, a psychoanalytic orientation that I have found impossible to eliminate, so embedded is this orientation in contemporary Western thought. My portrait of Tuhami bears less relationship to the traditional life histories based on the *Bildungsgeschichte* or to the conception of personal history in the novels of Balzac, Flaubert, and Zola (all of whom, I believe, have influenced the "life history" and the "case history") than it does to the modern novel that bespeaks the fragmented and alienated nature of its hero or anti-hero. Not only does Tuhami emerge as such, but, insofar as I can tell, so do I. My perspective changes in this book in ways that I was not always conscious of at the time of writing or editing. The narrative voice is limited, masked, devoid even of a constant perceptual and theoretical vantage point, and it is overwhelmingly self-conscious if not self-critical. An author, as Blanchot (1955) insists, is never capable of reading his own works.

•   •   •

As Tuhami's interlocutor, I became an active participant in his life history, even though I rarely appear directly in his recitations.* Not only did my presence, and my questions, prepare him for the text he was to produce, but they produced what I read as a change of consciousness in him. They produced a change of consciousness in me, too. We were both jostled from our assumptions about the nature of the everyday world and ourselves and groped for common reference points within this limbo of interchange. My research on the Hamadsha and my concern with Tuhami's personal history provided a frame, at least a cover (perhaps more for me than for Tuhami), for our interchange.

From the middle of March 1968, when I was first introduced to Tuhami, until the end of November of the same year, we met at least once a week. Our meetings, usually on Saturday mornings in my field assistant's house, lasted for three or four hours. My assistant, Lhacen, a Berber who did not normally live in Meknes,

---

*After finishing *Tuhami*, I came across Lawrence Watson's "Understanding a Life History as a Subjective Document" (1976), in which he takes into account the role of preunderstanding in the dialectical relationship that results in a life history. Watson's own hermeneutical and phenomenological perspective does not give sufficient attention to the several life-historical "texts" produced in that relationship and the constraints they impose. His conceptualization of the interlocutor in the construction of a life history needs elaboration.

was always present. The three of us would talk and drink heavily sweetened mint tea, which Tuhami, as the honored guest, would prepare. Occasionally Lhacen's three-year-old niece would come in and sit quietly on Tuhami's lap for the length of the interview. She adored Tuhami, and Tuhami was exquisitely gentle with her. He brought her amulets and other apotropaic devices to ward off the *jnun*, or demons, and gave Lhacen and his wife advice about her. He seemed far less interested in their own daughter, who was then only a few months old.

Lhacen liked Tuhami. He met him for the first time shortly after our arrival in Meknes. I had gone to Tangier to meet my wife, and, when I returned, Lhacen told me excitedly about the *informateur formidable* he had met in front of his new neighbor's house. (Lhacen and I had already been told about Tuhami by several other Moroccans.) Lhacen had even interviewed him! He respected Tuhami's knowledge of magic and healing, the lives of saints, the ways of demons, and the manners of men, and particularly, women; he was taken with his ability as a *raconteur*. He did recognize—and was puzzled by—Tuhami's peculiar character. The two of us discussed it at great length, and I am indebted to Lhacen for much of what I have to say about Tuhami. During our meetings, however, Lhacen made himself as unobtrusive as possible. Indeed, he had an extraordinary ability to efface himself when he acted as an interpreter, and Tuhami himself seemed to accept Lhacen's faceless presence with surprising ease. On occasion we both hid behind Lhacen's presence, but for the most part we talked to each other directly. As a Moroccan and yet a stranger to Meknes, and as a Berber, Lhacen provided, I believe, a "familiar distance" that was necessary for the frankness of our discourse. Had he not been there, our relationship would have been awkward. Present, he could be ignored and was ignored.*

Lhacen, like me, came to consider Tuhami a friend, but he never visited with Tuhami outside our meetings. I had in no way discouraged visits. If anything, I encouraged Lhacen to see the people I worked with whenever he could, and he often did. There was something, however, about the relationship that

---

*See Part Four for a more detailed account of Lhacen's role in the exchanges between Tuhami and me.

existed between Tuhami, Lhacen, and myself that precluded such meetings. It was as though Tuhami would—indeed, wanted to—reveal himself in interviews only if he could preserve a kind of potent privacy outside the interview situation. In part, I suppose, this privacy served to enhance his revelations and the aura of mystery about him. In part, too, it was a means of making the interviews exceptional, outside an everyday life in which a show of strength, *shih*, of dignity, of honor, had to be maintained. As it was for the pre-Islamic Arabs, honor—*'ird*—was for Tuhami, and other Moroccans, a partition, a curtain, a veil, with which he could separate himself from other people. Behind the veil were concealed precisely those personal characteristics, feelings, and concerns that, I must presume, Tuhami revealed in our interviews. Here, so to speak, he could lower his veil without subjecting himself to shame. (Both honor and shame have been held to be the principal regulators of social life in the Mediterranean world.) To have extended our relationship from the privileged domain of the interview to that of everyday life would have been too disrupting for Tuhami, and perhaps for me.

Initially I set out to question Tuhami about his involvement with the Hamadsha and other religious brotherhoods. I wanted to learn as much as I could about the significance of the order for nonmembers. I was anxious to learn not just what people said the order was about but the role it played in their articulation of experience, including their personal history. (I use the awkward phrase "in their articulation of experience" rather than simply "in their lives" to emphasize the fact that the information upon which such judgments are made is essentially verbal.) I encouraged, accordingly, reminiscence and free association. Tuhami responded with an ease of fantasy and self-reference that was not characteristic of the other Moroccans with whom I worked. Like them, he seldom asked me questions; he did manage to structure our meetings, as they frequently did, by selective hearing, by what sometimes appeared to me to be deliberate misunderstanding, and by wandering from the point of my questions as I saw them. He never missed a meeting without giving me a legitimate excuse ahead of time.

Tuhami was very much the storyteller and, talking to me, he used all of the storyteller's devices to create the effects he wanted. Encouraged by the ambiguity and the unfamiliarity of

our initial encounter and by my "neutrality" as an anthropologist, he permitted himself greater freedom of expression during our meetings than in the more structured encounters of everyday life. He was able, in other words, not only to
create the relationship he desired but to create me, for himself,
as well. I presented him with minimum resistance but, through
insistence and the direction of my questions, resistance all the
same.

Tuhami responded to our encounter, as I have said, with an
ease of fantasy and self-reference. It was often impossible to
distinguish what was real from what was dream and fantasy,
hallucination and vision. His interest was not in the informative
but in the evocative aspect of language. He contradicted himself
so often that even the minimum order I bestow on his life belies
its articulation. What I take to be real (and, at least heuristically,
I must take something in his discourse to be real) is my assumption.

At first Tuhami and I spoke mutually unintelligible languages.
I was primarily interested in information, Tuhami in evocation.
We did listen to each other, though, and soon our discourses
began to vacillate between the informative and the evocative. We
both tried to determine the direction: I with my prosaic questions, Tuhami, sometimes more extravagantly, with pro-
nouncements. I remember his beginning an interview once with
a kind of Delphic prophecy of World War III. He looked as if he
were not speaking; his eyes were focused somewhere far off in
the distance; his voice was deep and throaty; his words were
uttered with finality: "There will be trouble in Casablanca and
Rabat, then in Taza and Meknes. Fez alone will be spared. Tangier will be completely razed. There where there are houses,
plants will grow." More often he would begin by telling me a
dream—he knew I was interested in dreams—or by announcing
a decision to take a long trip. He never did.

Certain themes figured rhetorically in our interchange. Or,
rather, we used those themes rhetorically to preserve the interchange, whatever their personal significance may have been.
They became symbolic of our desire to maintain what I and, I
believe, Tuhami found captivating: mutual self-recognition. We
were, in this respect at least, friends.

One such theme, at first not explicitly stated, was Tuhami's marriage to the camel-footed she-demon 'A'isha Qandisha.* There was something fascinating about this demoness, quite apart from the role she played for the Hamadsha brotherhood and in the lives of many of the other Moroccans with whom I worked. Like the Indian goddess Kali-Parvati, she possessed two aspects: she could appear either as a hag—an archetypical phallic mother, with maenad-like curls, long pendulous breasts, and elongated nipples—or as a beauty with extraordinary seductive powers. She was, however, always a capricious, vindictive spirit, and she harshly controlled the lives of those men who succumbed to her. (The only way to resist her was to plunge an iron or steel knife into the earth when she approached.) Some, like Tuhami, were considered—and considered themselves— married to her; others were struck by her, and still others were possessed by her. The ultimate relationship was one of enslavement (cf. Crapanzano 1973). For me, of course, 'A'isha Qandisha represented the confrontation with the exotic, the bizarre, and the mad. She attested to my identity as an anthropologist and to my doing field work.

Tuhami recognized that 'A'isha Qandisha was different from, but no less real than, the ordinary human beings he encountered daily; she was simply real in a different way. I was at first tempted to dismiss her as a collectively sanctioned projection of some endopsychic disposition or conflict. Later, as I got to know Tuhami better and learned more about the role of 'A'isha Qandisha and other demons in the lives of many Moroccans, I came to question the applicability of the concept of projection, which, it seems to me, is based on a particular idiomatically determined conception of man and his motivations (Crapanzano 1977a). 'A'isha Qandisha and the other *jnun* are givens in the Moroccan's world; their givenness is periodically reconfirmed, however circularly, by the existence of illness and other extraordinary states immediately interpreted in terms of the *jnun* and of possession rites. These spirits are then elements in the idiom through which the Moroccan articulates his world (Crapanzano 1973, 1977c).

*Tuhami apparently told Lhacen on their first meeting that he had once seen 'A'isha Qandisha at her grotto near Sidi 'Ali's sanctuary in Beni Rachid. It was during the annual pilgrimage (see below, p. 96), and a group of women were deep in theriomimetic trance, groveling in the mud like pigs (Crapanzano 1973).

In Tuhami's Morocco the demonic elements are immediately
associated with maraboutism, the cult of saints, which is regarded as the hallmark of North African Islam (Dermenghem
1954). The Moroccan countryside is literally dotted with squat
white buildings with domed roofs, *qobbas*, where a saint, a *wali*, a
sayyid, a holy man endowed with great blessing, or *baraka*, is said
to be buried. Similar sanctuaries are found in every city; quarters are frequently named after them. Some, like the sanctuary
of Sidi Mohammed ben 'Isa—Shaykh el-Kamal, the Perfect
Shaykh—in Meknes are of international importance; others,
like that of Moulay Idriss on the Jebel Zerhoun, of national
importance; and still others, the majority, of significance only to
the members of a tribal segment or a village quarter.*

In some instances, as with Sidi Mohammed ben 'Isa and
Moulay Idriss, the saints are historical figures of considerable
reputation; in other instances they may be men and women
remembered, if at all, for their charisma, that "vividness" that
Clifford Geertz (1968) associates with the possession of *baraka*.
Some, like the Hamadsha saints, Sidi 'Ali ben Hamdush and Sidi
Ahmed Dghughi, are the subject of rich hagiographies—miracle
stories, really; others are remembered by name only. Some are
the founders of popular religious brotherhoods like those of the
Hamadsha and the 'Isawa; others began the elite, mystical confraternities, the Sufi orders, such as the Tijanniyya and the Nas-
siriyya. Some of the saints have descendants who care for their
sanctuaries and receive the gifts that are brought for their an-
cestors; others have left no one behind. "They, the saints, are

---

*Moroccans, including Tuhami, frequently speak of visiting a saint's sanctuary
as "visiting *the saint*," for they believe him to be alive in his sanctuary. For clarity I
have tried to differentiate the statements in which Tuhami seems to be referring
to the sanctuary from statements in which he is referring to the saint himself;
however, the essential ambiguity of his phrasing should be recognized in all of
his references to pilgrimages and visits to saints and their sanctuaries. In certain
instances—for example, when he talks about "going to Moulay Idriss"—there is
even greater ambiguity, for "Moulay Idriss" refers not only to the saint and to his
sanctuary but to the village in which his sanctuary is located, the village in which
he resides. (I have retained the French spelling *Moulay* instead of using *Mulay*,
which would have been more consistent with my system of transliteration; for
Moulay is the Moroccans' own preferred transliteration—the one they employ
when they refer, say, to the village of Moulay Idriss.)

like the branches of a tree," Tuhami once explained. "The Prophet is the trunk."

Associated with the saints is a gamut of rituals, ranging from the communal recitation of supernumerary prayers and highly stylized trance-dances to special massages with rocks endowed with *baraka*, baths in waters sacred to the saint, the removal of a handful of earth from the saintly sanctuary, or simply the circumambulation of the saint's tomb. Pilgrims frequently sleep in the sanctuary in the hope of having a dream; such dreams are thought to be messages from the saint or even visitations. Some Moroccans, like Tuhami, claim that the saints are alive in their tombs. For them the saints resemble rather more the *jnun* than deceased human beings. There is belief in neither ghosts nor ancestral spirits in Morocco.

The sanctuaries tend to be specialized, though never completely so. They may serve as a sacred arena for political and legal arbitrage or, like the churches of medieval Europe or the Buddhist shrines in Vietnam, as a place of political asylum. They are visited by pilgrims anxious for a cure for any ailment, ranging from a bout of rheumatism or menstrual cramps to demonic attack and spirit possession. They are visited, too, for poetic inspiration, acrobatic prowess, success in business or school, for the birth of a male child or the preservation of a marriage, or simply for those feelings of well-being that are associated with the gift of *baraka*. Most often, supplicant pilgrims promise to sacrifice something, a sheep, a goat, or perhaps a seven-colored chicken, or to give something, food, candles, or money to the saint, if he responds to their supplication. Such a pledge binds the supplicant to the saint, and failure to carry it out will result in great harm to him or his family; they will become vulnerable to the demons, for the saint will remove his protection if indeed he does not incite the *jnun* to attack.

The rituals and coordinate beliefs of the popular brotherhoods structure the relationship between saints, demons, and the human victim of demonic attack (Crapanzano 1973). The Hamadsha specialize in curing the victims of 'A'isha Qandisha and other female *jnun*. These *jinniyyas* are said to strike those who have offended or insulted them. (Usually the source of the injury is unknown to the victim.) The demons paralyze their victims, usually the left leg or arm or the left side of the face; they blind them, render them deaf or mute; they give them aching bones ("bones that pinch"), tingling sensations in their knees, wrists, and ankles, difficulties in breathing, menstrual cramps, or muscle pains; they cause them to suffer severe depressions or to experience a state of dissociation and *dédoublement de conscience,* which the Western psychiatrist would identify with hysterical, or even schizophrenic, dissociation and which the Hamadsha, and other Moroccans, diagnose as being inhabited or possessed by a demon. The *jnun* may often render a woman infertile or a man impotent, although impotence is seldom acknowledged publicly. The *jnun* themselves, however, are not evil. "They do not do bad things," Tuhami said. "If someone is all twisted up, it is his own fault and not Lalla 'A'isha's—or any other *jinn's*—fault. A woman goes to Lalla 'A'isha and promises her something if she has children. After she has children, she does not bring the gift she promised. Then Lalla 'A'isha will attack her." The *jnun,* like the saints, are angered when a promise is broken. They function at times like extrapolated superegos, externalized consciences, jealous embodiments of an often harsh and arbitrary sense of justice.

To be cured, the victim of the demon must satisfy his demon's desire. First, the demon's identity must be established and then his, or more often her, demands determined. A seer, or some other knowledgeable person, is called in for an opinion. Tuhami himself often served in this role, for he had immense knowledge of the demons, and my notes are filled with his long descriptions of Lalla Malika, Lalla Mimuna, Lalla Mira, and, of course, Lalla 'A'isha. Sometimes affecting a state of partial dissociation, sometimes in fact in trance, the seer hyperventilates over a brazier of smoking incense and prescribes a course of action that usually involves visiting one or more saints in the area. (Tuhami neither feigned trance nor went into one; he was an advisor and not a seer.) If the visits do not work, then a Hamadsha cure, or the cure offered by another brotherhood, will be suggested.

Cures by the popular religious brotherhoods are sought as a last resort, for they are expensive. Not only must the host help pay the curers for the ceremony; he must also provide a meal for all those who attend it. Often, in the poor quarters of Meknes that Tuhami frequented, a hundred or more guests would gather for the *hadra,* or trance-dance. The victim—as well as other devotees of the order—is danced into a deep trance called *jidba,* which is thought to be pleasing to the attacking demon. He loses control of himself; he may fall to the ground in a cataleptic seizure; he may beckon seductively to the musical instruments, drums, oboes, recorders, and guitars; he may rub himself against other dancers; or he may mutilate himself. The Hamadsha are notorious for slashing their scalps with knives or, on special occasions, with halberds, but I have also seen them cut at their forearms, drink boiling water, sit on a brazier of burning coals, eat glass, or knock their heads against a wall with extraordinary violence. One dancer described his condition in the following words:

> I am hot and breathe heavily. I feel myself throbbing. There is much itching. I am not conscious of my body. I do not know where I am. Nor do I know what time it is. My body feels like boiling water. It is frightening. I see only 'A'isha. . . . It is 'A'isha who makes me hit my head. I see her in front of me. She has a piece of iron. She is hitting her head. There is itching and sweating, and my whole body is hot. When 'A'isha stops hitting, so do I. Then I continue to dance. [Crapanzano 1973]

When the dancer has danced to the satisfaction of his *jinn,* he sits down among the guests and eats ravenously at the communal feast that ends the ceremony. If the dance has been a success, he sleeps well and wakes revitalized. Whatever the symptoms that necessitated the invitation, they are now alleviated if not totally removed.

The cure itself is interpreted as an appeasement of the demon, usually a she-demon, by means of the saint's blessing. It is the *baraka* of the saint that enables the victim of demonic attack to enter trance and become possessed. It is the she-demon who is held responsible for extreme behavior in *jidba.* Once she has been appeased, she not only releases her victim but becomes his protector as well. As long as he obeys her commands—wearing certain colors, burning special incense, making periodic trips to her sanctuary and the sanctuaries of her favored saints, dancing to music that is pleasing to her, and, to be sure, sponsoring commemorative ceremonies—the she-demon will keep him in good health and fortune. If, however, he should neglect her, he will suffer the same symptoms, often in a more virulent form, that first required cure.

The saints and demons, their ways and wiles, their needs and desires, can never be fully understood by man. Such understanding lies with Allah alone. A man's fate rests with Allah; his destiny is written. It partakes of the sacred. A man, as Tuhami explained it, can only remain sincere in his intention (*niyya*) and act from his heart. This "writtenness" of the universe is an implicit component of Tuhami's thought. It provides the limit to his explanations of the chain of events that constitute the history of his world as he had learned it and knows it. It gives to this chain of events a certain weight—an almost sacred givenness independent of individual initiative—that provides a ground for the awe he feels before the world in its historical immensity. This writtenness justifies, too, his resignation to the past, his past, and to a future that he envisions with a pessimist's foreboding.

Tuhami, however, like other Moroccans, is not usually given to rationalizing his failures, his disappointments, his plight, in terms of Allah's will. He is rather the victim of the *jnun* and the saints. Both serve in an intermediate position between the more distant, the more philosophical, the ultimate horizon of fate, and the more immediate, the more tangible, the personal limit of individual initiative and enterprise—between the transcendental plane of a godhead that verges in its impersonality on the otiose and the mundane plane of reality that is perhaps overpersonalized, certainly overburdened with human responsibility. The *jnun* and the saints give escape to Tuhami. They enable a radical shift of responsibility, of motivational locus, from self to Other, from who he is to who he is not. There is, however, always a transcendental factor responsible for displacement. Impersonal, empty, and even, as Hegel would maintain, universal, we in the West call this factor desire and give it, at least today, a "psychological" locus.

Some phenomenologically influenced sociologists, like Peter Berger and Thomas Luckmann (1967), have suggested that the psychological theories at the disposal of an individual realize themselves in his experience.

If a psychology becomes socially established (that is, becomes generally recognized as an adequate interpretation of objective reality), it tends to realize itself forcefully in the phenomena it purports to interpret. Its internalization is accelerated by the fact that it pertains to internal reality, so that the individual realizes it in the very act of internalizing it. [P. 178]

I have suggested this, too (1973, 1975)—and suggest it here—but with one caveat. What the ethnographer or the psychologist is provided with is either an immediate or a mediate verbal text and not a direct access to the mind of his informant or subject. The extent to which such texts accurately report the experience they purport to describe, the extent to which they "realize" themselves in the experience, must inevitably remain open questions. They must not be dismissed, as some of the behaviorists have dismissed them (with a vehemence that is somewhat suspect), nor should they be ignored, as some of the more soft-minded humanistic psychologists have done by the simple assumption that what a subject says he has experienced is, in fact, what he experienced. In our everyday transactions we act, indeed we must act, as though the experience an individual reports is, in fact, the experience he experienced, unless of course he is being duplicitous or self-deceptive. In other words, in everyday life we collapse the conceptualization and the phenomenology of experience. Without entering here into questions of the temporality of experience—immediate utterances versus retrospective accounts—it is important to recognize that the two, the conceptualization and the phenomenology of experience, must be analytically separated if an epistemologically valid science of man is to be achieved.

Experiences that the Westerner would conceptually locate within himself and would call "inner," "mental," or "psychological" the Moroccan may well conceptualize within the demonic idiom as outside himself (Crapanzano 1977a). What the Westerner would call a guilty conscience, for example, might be articulated in terms of demonic interference. Indeed, extreme rage, excessive courage (the Roman warrior's *furor*), poetic and other inspirational states, sexual attraction, love, various compulsive and obsessional conditions, fear, and other dispositions that the Westerner might describe in terms of being "beside himself"—a legacy, perhaps, of a past demonic idiom—are often described by the Moroccan in terms of possession by 'A'isha Qandisha or some other spirit. The boundaries of self, of inner and outer life, and the source and location of motivation—or desire, the word I prefer—must be recognized as essentially metaphorical.

·   ·   ·

The status granted the metaphor (and the idiomatic elements) reflects the implicit ontological assumptions of the idiom. When Tuhami talks of 'A'isha Qandisha and other demons, the Westerner is tempted to treat these demons as collectively sanctioned products of Tuhami's imagination, as "projections" or "collective representations," that are somehow not quite "real." He will look to "reality" to understand them without questioning the status of that "reality." 'A'isha Qandisha and the other demons may be regarded, accordingly, as refractions of "social processes," "tensions within the society," "conflicts within the individual," "guilt," "libidinal impulses," "archetypical propensities," or, on a slightly more concrete level, "historical events." The choice of explanatory ground is, of course, dependent upon the particular theoretical stance accepted; the ground itself is a reification of an essentially abstract concept or category, of a symbol or idiomatic element, which, if one stops to think about it, is no more or less "real" than the demonic elements in Tuhami's discourse. As Vivian Garrison (1977) has quite appropriately pointed out in her study of spirit possession among Puerto Ricans in New York City, the spirits are explanatory concepts. The difference is perhaps simply that in the one instance the Westerner is willing to accept the conspiratorial reification that provides him with a satisfying explanation, but in the other he is unwilling to enter the conspiracy. Tuhami would probably be equally unwilling to enter the Western conspiracy.

When Tuhami talks about people such as the pasha's son, his wives, and his own mother and father, the Westerner will be tempted to accept them as "real," as I did. He will not easily recognize that for Tuhami, at least in his conversations with me, such "real" persons were metaphorical; they served, as did the demons, a symbolic interpretive function. It is for this reason that I begin this portrait of Tuhami with a tale that resists integration into his life story and yet bears on its truth. Like so many of those fragments of information through which anthropologists come to understand the culture or the people they study and which they can never incorporate into their ethnographies, Tuhami's tale of the pasha's son revealed to me the presumption of our collapsing the real and the true. In the pages that follow, the reader will find that the themes expressed in Tuhami's tale of the pasha's son recur again and again in his recitations. They are expressed in different registers: the historical, the demonic, the magical, and the folkloristic. They express the abandon of a boy, the arbitrariness of the man, the manipulation of the woman, the desire for a family. They express, too, those most human concerns: love and death, warmth and security, honor and shame, the maintenance of personal integrity within the scheming and intriguing of social life, the need for escape and transcendence, for meaning. And, above all, they express the desire to be special, to be an *individual* within the collectivity, a desire that has so often been denied to the "primitive" by the "nonprimitive," who wishes the anguish of identity for himself alone.

I am not suggesting here that the Westerner's scientific explanations and Tuhami's symbolic interpretive explanations are equally satisfying. That is for the reader to decide on the basis of criteria he finds acceptable. (The criteria themselves are, of course, idiomatically constrained!) I am simply asking the reader to abandon for the moment his assumptions about reality and his ground of explanation as he reads through the following pages. That way he will share, I hope, some of the anguished puzzlement I felt, and presumably Tuhami felt, as we tried to make sense of each other. Tuhami will speak directly; he will not share my self-reflective stance. His reflection must inevitably remain a silent undersong to his discourse. His text, too, however accurately I can present it, is in a sense my text. I have assumed it and afforded myself, as narrator, a privilege he has not been granted. I have had the privilege of (re)encounter. I hope, however, that through my assumption the reader will discover Tuhami and recognize in him something of himself. The Sufis say that transcendence comes when one discovers oneself in the Other and, in the idiom of the West, does not merely project oneself into the Other to discover, *mirabile dictu,* only oneself there.

Part One

Part One

Tuhami was, as I have said, an illiterate Moroccan Arab. He was a tilemaker by trade, and he lived alone in a windowless hovel in the factory where he worked for day wages, along with eight other men. The factory was a complex of gray-ochre and whitewashed buildings, located, as if symbolically, below the bridge that crosses the river Bu Fekran, the Father of the Tortoises, now a trickling stream, which divides the old quarter, the *medina,* of Meknes from the European quarter, the Ville Nouvelle, as it is often called by even those who know no French.* In the vicinity of the bridge, Tuhami told me, live forty-four saints, the *rjal el-bled,* who protect him and other pious people who know about them from the evils that befall man. In the river, whose waters are not very clean, women come to wash wool and sheepskin rugs. Tuhami bathes in the river when he is quite alone. The bridge and the dusty, tarred road that crosses it, joining the old and new towns of Meknes, separate the factory from a much larger whitewashed factory, now more or less defunct, that was once owned by a family I will call the Jolans, *colons* of French and Spanish origin who came to Meknes, I believe, by way of Algeria.

Both factories have a shabby, deteriorated look about them. Like the rest of the city, they attest to former glory. Tuhami claims, on pseudo-etymological grounds, that Meknes was

---

*Official policy under the first French resident general, Marshal Lyautey, and his town planner, Henri Prost, was to separate the new European quarters of Moroccan cities from their old *medinas* in order to protect the autonomy of each. No plans were made for the possible expansion of the Moroccan quarters (Dethier 1973), which, according to ben Jelloun (1979), became a symbol of *la vie archaïque et rétrograde* for the Moroccan bourgeoisie. Today they are vastly overpopulated, greatly deteriorated, and, again according to ben Jelloun, ghettos for the poor and miserable.

founded by a people, *nas*, from Mecca. Once, in fact, a series
of Berber villages along the bank of the Bu Fekran (called at
the time of Oued Felfel the River of Red Pepper), Meknes
became a provincial city under the great dynasties of Morocco.
In the seventeenth century it was developed into a grandiose
capital by the Alawite Sultan Moulay Isma'il, who was famous in
Europe for his extravagant palaces and his dungeons full of
Christian slaves. In Morocco he is remembered for his
ironhanded rule, his promiscuous beheadings, and his extraordinary virility. His palaces, built, torn down, and continually
rebuilt during the fifty-three years of his reign, are mostly in
ruins today. Their nooks and crannies are occupied by poor
squatters, *fellahin*, from the countryside, who poured into the
city with the arrival of the French. They settled where they
could, first in the crowded *medina* and then in the vast shantytowns that began to spring up in the mid-1930s outside the
city walls and beyond the cemeteries (Franchi 1959).

The European quarter has also deteriorated. The houses
there—some, in the suburb of Plaisance, as pretentious as any
Scarsdale minicastle, others as ordinary as the pastel villas of the
postwar *banlieux* of any Mediterranean city—have been ne-
glected by their new Moroccan owners, who took them over at
Independence in 1956 and who, for the most part, have neither
the money nor the inclination to maintain them properly. The
broad avenues and open intersections, which contrast so sharply
with the narrow, winding streets and alleys and the claustrophobic squares of the *medina*, are lined with dilapidated
shops, *parfumeries, librairies, quincailleries,* and the rare boutiques
that survived the exodus of the *colons*. These shops are under-
stocked, and, when they are stocked, it is with seconds, factory
rejects, and those inferior products that the big European,
American, and Japanese manufacturers unload on Third World
markets. On their back shelves are still to be found occasional
remnants of pre-Independence prosperity: an unusual book, a
fine champagne, long since dead, a bolt of subtly patterned silk,
a superb knife or rifle, an evening gown now completely out of
fashion, or even a toothbrush made of expensive boar bristles.
The *confiserie-pâtisserie*, which in 1968 was still owned by a local
French family, was deserted at teatime, and it now used vegeta-
ble oil instead of butter in its cakes. What restaurants there were

still preferred the inevitable provincial menu of *entrecôte,
pommes-frites, haricots-verts,* and *crème-caramel* to couscous, *tajin* (a
stew), and other Moroccan foods. And the movie theaters—
there were several large ones in the Ville Nouvelle—were all in
need of paint and new seats and smelled of dry sweat and urine.
They showed Italian and Spanish Westerns and violent
whodunits. In 1968 the judo and karate films had not yet arrived
from the Orient.

Once a thriving agricultural center, bordered by the fertile
plains of the Gharb and Zerhoun area, Meknes was in a state of
economic stagnation when I lived there. It was considered, however, by most Moroccans to be the *most* Moroccan of the imperial
cities of the kingdom. It was known not only for the ruins of
Moulay Isma'il's palaces, for his great portals, the Bab Jdid, the
Bab Berdain, and the Bab Khemis, and for its many splendid
mosques but also for its healthy air (there is a sanitorium in
Meknes), its fresh produce, and the tempered violence of its
inhabitants. At the turn of the century, according to Budgett
Meakin (1901), a long-time resident of Morocco whose father
founded the *Moroccan Times,* it had "the worst possible reputation for morals, rivaling Sodom and Gomorrah in the tales of
wickedness." It had been a garrison for Moulay Isma'il and then
for the French, as today it is a garrison for the Moroccan army.
It lay on the great East-West caravan route, the *tariq s-sultan,* and
was—and still is—an important market town for the Arabs of the
plains and the Berbers of the mountains. Despite the monu-
mentality of its ruined palaces, gates, and walls, Meknes retains a
distinctly rural character, which perhaps accounts for the fact
that it is so highly regarded by so many Moroccans. To the
European or American it looks like a dilapidated agricultural
town.

Meknes has been known by travelers from time immemorial
for its muddy streets and the exceptional jealousy of its men. In
the sixteenth century Leo Africanus (1956) wrote that "The
wives of gentlemen do not leave their homes except at night.
Their faces are covered, and they do not want to be seen either
veiled or unveiled, because the men are very jealous and even
dangerous when it comes to their women" (p. 177). Meakin
(1901) also observed that the men of Meknes are known for their
bravery and that their women "are famed throughout Morocco

for their beauty," which, he adds, "is not, however, of the type to captivate Europeans." Today the respectable women of Meknes rarely leave their homes unaccompanied. The veil is still worn—a bit sloppily, to be sure, and below the nose—by many young women, and it is not unusual to see a schoolgirl dressed one day in a short skirt and the next in the camouflage of the traditional *jallaba*. Prostitutes also wear the traditional *jallaba* and veil, usually in bright colors. Their hoods, at least in 1968, were pointed. Some of them wore white gloves, almost as a professional symbol.

The women of Meknes, like the women of Morocco more generally, are considered, at least by men, to be inferior to men, essentially lacking in control over their sexual impulses, adventure-seeking, and always fair game when alone. They are associated, the Moroccan feminist author Fatima Mernissi (1975) observes, with *fitna*, with chaos and disorder. *Fitna* refers not only to chaos, disorder, political agitation, rioting, distraction, perturbation, torment, and panic but also to women (Mercier 1951). In its verbal form it means to "pester," "incite," "agitate," "bewitch," and "bedazzle," Women are conceived, then, according to Mernissi, as a threat to the Moroccan male's sense of self and self-control:

> The Muslim Woman is endowed with a fatal attraction which erodes the male's will to resist her and reduces him to a passive acquiescent role. He has no choice; he can only give in to her attraction, whence her identification with *fitna*, chaos, and with the anti-divine and anti-social forces of the universe. [Mernissi 1975, p. 11]

Moroccan folk wisdom is permeated with a negative attitude toward women. The attraction for women is associated with Shitan, Satan, or one of his refractions. Mernissi quotes the sixteenth-century poet Sidi 'Abderrahman El Mejdoub as offering "the best example" of the distrust of women.

> Women's intrigues are mighty.
> To protect myself I never stop running.
> Women are belted with serpents
> And bejeweled with scorpions.

This "phallic-aggressive" imagery is, of course, also characteristic of 'A'isha Qandisha and other *jinniyya*.

Given this stereotype, women are presumed to require the strictest vigilance. The Moroccan world, like other North African and Middle Eastern worlds, is split dramatically into the women's world of hearth and home and the man's world of mosque and marketplace. Although a Moroccan man may enter or leave his home as he pleases, a Moroccan woman has no such freedom. Before marriage she is under the surveillance of her parents and brothers. Her sexual fidelity, a mark of family honor, must be safeguarded not only by her husband but by her ubiquitous mother-in-law. (Marriages in Morocco are usually virilocal.) She must ask permission to go to the *hammam*, the steam baths—reputed, at least among men, to be a place where illicit meetings are arranged—and to visit saints' sanctuaries. Women are not permitted in mosques and do not usually go to the market. In the shantytowns of Meknes that Tuhami frequented, they do occasionally do the marketing, bring bread to the public ovens, and fetch water. They are veiled and are accompanied, whenever possible, by a woman past menopause, who is considered to be without sexual allure and is thus allowed greater freedom. Women past menopause are often suspected of witchcraft.

[margin note: women past menopause]

The relations between spouses are fragile. Marriages are arranged by mothers, and the bride-price and marriage contract are negotiated by fathers. The bride and groom do not ordinarily meet before the wedding night. The wedding itself may be an elaborate ceremony lasting as long as a week or, today, especially among the urban poor, a simple affair lasting little more than a day. It is, in either case, a very tense occasion, for not only is the honor of both families at stake but a considerable financial sacrifice is required of both as well. The ceremony culminates in the groom's defloration of his bride, and the guests wait expectantly for proof of the bride's virginity. The bride's mother or mother-in-law rushes in as soon as possible to inspect the wedding cloth for blood and then dances out to the guests, bearing it on a tea tray on her head. (What is not spoken of but must surely be acknowledged is that the blood-stained cloth is also a sign of the groom's potency.) The bride's position in her new family is that of a suspect outsider who must be "domesticated." Her position improves somewhat after she has borne a son, but she lives, nevertheless, under the threat of divorce (she herself cannot normally initiate a divorce) and under the domination of her

[margin note: Truly amazing]

mother-in-law. Her husband, humble before his father, gives his primary loyalty to his mother. Mernissi (1975) stresses the claustrophobic absence of privacy within the Moroccan household.

The image of women that Tuhami presents in the pages that follow is, then, by no means exceptional. It is a stereotype, frozen in time and context, perhaps stimulated by my presence and Lhacen's, and as such it is inadequate to the actual ongoing intricate relations between Moroccan men and women. It does not do justice, save implicitly, perhaps through a conspiratorial silence, to the changing images women present over the course of a lifetime (Dwyer 1978). (One of the characteristics of stereotypic thinking is the reduction of movement through time to a symbolic instant that is perhaps psychologically satisfying to the thinker but is rarely sufficient to the subject of his thought.) Within the prevailing image of women in Morocco—an image the women themselves often accept as a *reality*—is a changing evaluation from positive to negative, which is reflected in the common belief that women are born with a hundred angels and men with a hundred devils and that over a lifetime the angels move to the men and the devils to the women (Dwyer 1978 and several of my informants). The essentially negative image of women refers principally to sexually mature women. As Daisy Dwyer (1978) notes, Adam and Eve were equals in the Garden of Eden. (They are not equals, however, in the vision of the afterlife that I learned from Tuhami and other Moroccans.) The negative image is of course rhetorically manipulated among men, as between Tuhami and me, and presumably among women, for a host of reasons, not the least of which is one of sensationalism. It should, however, be evaluated, as Dwyer (1978) points out, in terms of a frequently negative image of men and an almost existential cynicism, generally, about the nature of human beings and their relationships. Its appeal to the Westerner, particularly to the Western man, should be questioned, as both Dwyer (1978) and Said (1978) argue.

Tuhami was reputed for his knowledge of the ways of women. He was known among the women themselves, those of the shantytowns and poorer quarters of Meknes, for his herbal remedies, magical brews, and tales of saints and demons. Women respected him for his advice, which he often gave in oracular fashion. Men tended to ignore him. They called him *makhardil*, "scatterbrained" (the Arabic word suggests dissociation, flight of ideas, absentmindedness), and I have heard at least one man jokingly call him an *'aguza*, an "old woman," a "hag," a "witch." Men—and this is most unusual—did not particularly object when he entertained their women late into the night with his tales and lore. They did not find him threatening.

Tuhami was probably in his middle forties. His exact age was impossible to determine, since Moroccans of his background do not keep track of their birth dates. He claimed to be fifty-five, but this seems unlikely. He had distinctly negroid features. He was a very dark-skinned, thin man, perhaps five feet, five inches tall, with a puffed-out barrel chest and a slight steatopygia. His head was very round, shiny, and almost bald—something unusual for a Moroccan of his age—and his baldness troubled him greatly. He considered it to be a sign of age and ugliness, especially unappealing to women. Except when he was working in the factory in his ragged gray chemise, he always dressed in faded blue pants, which no longer buttoned at the fly, a bright blue sweater, a discarded jacket from someone else's suit, and a pair of old sneakers. That was his uniform. He never wore a *jallaba*, he said, because he never had the money to buy one. He was immaculately clean, and his nails were always well trimmed. He was patient and inspired calm.

Tuhami was a very gentle man, immediately likable, soft-spoken, and not much given to the kind of gesturing with which most Moroccans punctuate their speech. There was nothing effeminate about him. He had bright brown eyes, and, when he was happy, his large yellow upper front teeth (his lower front teeth were missing) were always showing in a huge, friendly smile; but when he was morose, he would sit alone in a corner of his windowless hovel, lost in himself and in the demons around him, the *jnun*, whom he alone could see and hear and about whom he could not speak. Or he would walk, often for miles, to a saint's tomb, a sanctuary, which he had dreamed of or fantasied, in the hope that the saint's blessing, his *baraka*, would free him from his depression. (He was a good Muslim, a pious man who recited his prayers daily, attended the Friday mosque services, and fasted not just during the month of Ramadan, as required by both Muslim and Moroccan law, but during the preceding

month of Sha'ban as well.) Occasionally Tuhami would go to the
movies—to lurid Indian romances or, less frequently, to violent
Westerns—to rid himself of his sadness. The movies were of
little help unless he could recast them as personal tales and use
them to captivate an audience. His depressions were not in his
control but in that of 'A'isha Qandisha and still other demons,
often more demanding, certainly more menacing, I was to learn,
than his *jinn*-bride.

· · ·

Tuhami was born in the late 1920s or early '30s in a desolate
village near Sidi Kacem on the great arid wheat plains of north-
ern Morocco. Like most Moroccans, he knew little of his family's
past; there were no heroes, no brigands, saints, or warriors, who
rose out of the monotony of centuries of tilling the same soil.
There was no affiliation, real or putative, to one of the
thousands of sherifian lineages, extending back to the Prophet
Mohammed, that are so often claimed in the Muslim world.
There was no justification for genealogical depth, no particular
merit in the ancestor. Tuhami's genealogy went back only two
generations.

Family extends through time by repetition—a repetition without episodic significance. Children are born and named on the
seventh day. Boys' hair is first cut at a saint's tomb and left there.
They are circumcised later; there is a feast. They tend the flocks,
learn to till the fields and harvest the crops. They avoid their
fathers and their fathers' domination. They sleep with one
another, the older boy mounting the younger, and are married
not by their choice but according to custom or their fathers'
wishes. During the wedding celebration itself their fathers avoid
any direct contact with them. Fathers sit with friends in a separate room, away from the female dancers and musicians. Sons
become fathers, members of their village councils; but it is not
until their own fathers die that they feel themselves truly men.
They, too, die. Occasionally one will have left the village for the
city, in search of wealth, or will have followed the route of the
beggar-pilgrim, hopeful of reaching Mecca but seldom actually
going further than one of the greater saintly sanctuaries.

Girls, following their mothers about, learn to cook and sew

and manage a household quietly and unostentatiously, and they hear the secrets of womanhood—of birth, the raising of children, menstruation, cures for illness, and magical spells to counter the domination of their men and the fragility of their marriages. They are separated from their brothers, who are, nevertheless, morally and legally responsible for them, and from other boys and men, and they are married soon after they experience the first flow of menstrual blood. No ceremony commemorates their menarche. They give birth to children, preferably to boys, watch half their children die, and suffer their husbands' perfunctory performance of their marital rights. They die. Occasionally one will have had to leave, disgraced, for the city, there to become a whore, for there is no other choice for the disgraced woman. Transcendence—escape—comes to some of them, and to some of their husbands, through the ecstasy of the trance-dance. This is not without cost, for it opens to them the dangerous world of the *jnun.*

Repetition is enveloped in a greater history, of which Tuhami was only dimly aware. This history is really closer to myth and legend. Desire is inhibited less by "reality" than by idiom. Chronology is of little significance; birth dates are ignored. Events centuries—and miles—apart are merged. The Prophet, an 'Umayyad caliph, a Persian prince, Moulay Idriss, and a local holy man who died fifty or a hundred years ago live as contemporaries in the same world. Even with the arrival of the French at the turn of this century—and of the Spaniards, further north—a historical consciousness did not necessarily develop. (Tuhami remembered no stories of the arrival of the French in his village.) The Europeans brought with them the greater possibilities of the modern world and also the contingencies that mask, if they do not destroy, the cycles of repetition. But such contingencies provide only the possibility of history; they do not necessarily bring it about. An ontological reevaluation is required; idiom must give way to reality as the primary restriction on desire in the articulation of the past. Resistance is met, for such a past is, of course, less secure.

Tuhami's parents and grandparents were farm workers, *fellahin.* They worked on the estates of wealthy Moroccan landowners who lived in Fez and Rabat. Tuhami's father, Driss, and his paternal grandfather M'hamid, were members of the Shrarda

tribe. Tuhami remembered little of them. He did remember
listening to his father's mother, Khadija, tell of the time of *siba*,
of dissidence, when there were still tribes that resisted government taxation and control. She held women responsible for the
wars of the past. She was a midwife who delivered eighty-five
babies, all of whom lived, approaching the magical hundred that
would guarantee her entry into Paradise. She lived, Tuhami
said, to be one hundred sixty years old.

Fatima, Tuhami's mother, considered herself to be a member
of the neighboring Hajawa tribe. In fact, her father, Moulay
'Abdeslem—Tuhami's maternal grandfather—came from Marrakech. He was black-skinned. His family was from the Tafilelt,
in the Sahara, and was probably brought north from sub-
Saharan Africa by slave traders. Moulay 'Abdeslem married
Fatima's mother, Dawia, who was a Hajawa, after completing a
tour of duty in the war against the Rifian nationalist 'Abdel Krim
in the 1920s. Dawia was Moulay 'Abdeslem's fourth wife, and,
well after her death, he married again (Moulay 'Abdeslem was
by then "one hundred fifty years old," according to Tuhami). He
lived with his new wife for a few months and then divorced her,
irritably blaming Tuhami, by then an orphan, for coming
around too often for food.

Dawia was a midwife, too. She moved to Meknes with her
husband, who, as a Marrakchi, a city-dweller, would not live in
the country, and bore him three daughters and a son. Moulay
'Abdeslem made baskets and straw mats; Dawia wove rugs. She
joined the 'Isawa brotherhood and fell into their most violent
trance. Like the Bacchantes of ancient Greece, she threw herself
on live sheep and goats, tore them apart with her hands and
teeth, and gorged herself on their still-hot raw flesh (Brunel
1926). Tuhami as a child was made to watch this spectacle. His
mother, Fatima, danced on occasion with the Hamadsha, and
Tuhami was made to watch their head-slashing too. No other
member of his family ever joined a religious brotherhood.

With the exception of Fatima, all of Moulay 'Abdeslem's and
Dawia's children settled in the city: Fatima's elder sister, Yemna,
in Meknes, and her younger sister and brother, Hadda and 'Abdelkader, in Casablanca. The two sisters, Yemna and Hadda,
married men who served in the French army; 'Abdelkader was
still unmarried in 1968. Fatima married Driss and moved to the

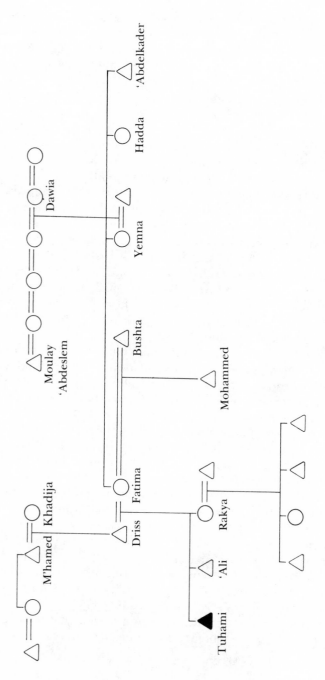

TUHAMI'S GENEALOGY

country. (Tuhami was, by convention, unable to tell me the circumstances of his parents' marriage.) Fatima gave birth to Tuhami in the country—her mother-in-law, Khadija, assisting—
and to his brother, 'Ali, and his sister, Rakya, at her sister's in
Meknes. Dawia probably assisted at their birth.

Tuhami's parents did not move to Meknes until Tuhami
was eight or nine, but Fatima and the children seem to have
spent considerable time there with Yemna before their actual move. It was Yemna's husband's promise to find work for
Driss that finally convinced him to move to Meknes himself. The
family settled into a single room with a little court in the same
range that housed Yemna and some forty other families. The
range was located in Foqharin, one of Meknes' shantytowns.
Driss could thank his sister-in-law and her husband for finding
him quarters in a white clay-brick range, built by the French,
rather than in one of the more usual shanties made of old tin
cans, tar paper, scraps of wood, and wattle and daub where most
newcomers to the city lived. However small, his quarters offered
some protection against the summer heat and the damp cold of
the Moroccan winters. Its floors, at least, did not turn to mud
during the winter rains.

Driss found work in a nearby quarry and, shortly after that, he
died. Tuhami stated this coldly, matter-of-factly, as though his
father's death meant nothing to him. He had used the same tone
when he told me, the first time I met him, that his parents moved
to Meknes when he was little and that now the *bled*, the countryside, meant nothing to him. It was about this time, Tuhami
claimed, that the pasha's son took him to work for him.

What ties Tuhami had with his father, his father's family, his
patrilineage, his *bled* (the Moroccan word has a spiritual connotation that is not covered even by the English "homeland" [cf.
Rabinow 1975]) were gone. His paternal grandparents were
already dead, and his father's only sibling was a sister who had
married into another family in another Shrarda village. He was
deprived not only of a parental model, however distant, but of
the economic and emotional security that a father and his family
give. A son in Morocco is *in a very real sense* an extension of his
father. His father's seed alone creates him; his mother serves
only as its receptacle; for, according to Tuhami, it is molded by
angels into a human infant. More important, he was deprived of

the social orientation, the developmental vector toward manhood, and the symbolic matrix for self-definition and world-construction that patrilineal affiliation provides to the Moroccan male.

Tuhami was left with a mother, a younger brother, and a sister, none of whose demands he could meet. As father surrogates, he had men—Moulay 'Abdeslem, Yemna's husband, and, later, a stepfather—with whom he was associated only through his mother.* At times he called himself Tuhami ben Moulay 'Abdeslem, but this use of his maternal grandfather's name as his patronymic was an inauthentic subterfuge. Neither Moulay 'Abdeslem nor the other men with whom he was associated through his mother could offer him manhood or even its possibility. He would have to seek his manhood *elsewhere:* among the saints.

• • •

— My mother was still young when my father died. People told her to get married again. She did. Her new husband never accepted me. I left the house. I went to work for a Frenchwoman, Mme Jolan. I worked and slept there.

— Why weren't you accepted?

— There were three of us. He could not take care of us all. I was the eldest.

— What did your mother say to this?

— My mother did not have time to say stay or don't stay. I left right away.

There was scorn in Tuhami's voice and gesture. Several months later, he elaborated on his feelings.

— I was angry, I didn't want her to marry. That is why her husband didn't want me around. I was always screaming at him and insulting him—slamming the door in his face.

— Were you angry at your mother?

— No.

— Why?

*The early end of patrilineal ties and the closeness Tuhami felt for his mother's family probably account for a definite and unusual matrilineal bias in his account not only of his own family history but, later, that of the Jolan family.

— It was Shitan who wanted my mother to marry. My mother was working. I was working too. There was no point in her marrying. If she wanted sex, all she had to do was go out and get it and come back.

The displacement of motivation to Shitan, the Muslim Satan (whom Moroccans hold responsible for sexual misdemeanors), is unsatisfactory. Moroccan sons do not refer to their mothers' sexuality. Tuhami's suggestion that his mother should satisfy herself with anyone was a mark of extreme contempt. Despite his denial, Tuhami was clearly very angry at his mother. It was she who abandoned him.

Tuhami's attitude toward his stepfather, Bushta, was more realistic. (Bushta was a soldier and a friend of Yemna's husband.) Tuhami meant nothing to Bushta. Bushta's rejection of him was something to be expected. What responsibility did Bushta have for the boy? He was taking in two children as it was. He had to be practical; there was little enough for himself, his wife, and her two children. Bushta meant nothing to Tuhami. And yet he was almost Tuhami's father. He was the man who took Tuhami's mother away. The door had to be slammed on him. Tuhami did not mention him when he gave me his genealogy or when he corrected it. He even claimed that his stepbrother, Mohammed, was his real brother. He never called Bushta by name. (The name is my invention.)

— Did your mother help you find work?
— No. A man helped get me work. He was in charge of Mme Jolan's workers. My mother thought I was walking the streets and doing nothing. (*Tuhami looked disgusted.*) Then one day she saw the workers lined up for pay. I was there too. She went up to the foreman and asked him if Monsieur Tuhami was working there. He said I was. She thanked him and explained that her husband wouldn't have me. People kept telling me to visit my parents, but I said, "Never." (*Tuhami emphasized the "never" with a sweep of his hand.*)

What Tuhami failed to mention was that his mother was Mme Jolan's cook and that she lived near the Jolan tile factory. She must have known that her son was working there.

On another occasion Tuhami describes how he had to fend for himself.

— I stayed with them [his mother and stepfather] for a month, and then it was finished. . . . Then I ran off without saying a word.
— What happened the day you ran away?
— Nothing. (*Tuhami was very evasive.*) I saw that my stepfather didn't want to feed me. (*He paused.*)
— Do you remember the first night away from home?
— I was just walking. I didn't know where I was going. Suddenly I met someone who asked me where I was going. I told him I didn't know. He asked if I wanted to be a shepherd. I said I did. I spent seven nights at his house. I wasn't going to work for him but for someone else. He called a neighbor, and he told her I could be her shepherd. She kissed his hand. He said, "Here is the boy, but you have to take care of him." I went to my new boss's house. She gave me a *jallaba,* pants, and a shirt. "You have three days here at the house to do nothing," she said. "Walk around! Play! Eat!" On the fourth day she gave me forty-five cows to take to the ravine. I took them and sat down all alone. I always led them to where there was a lot of grass. Everyone was saying how good Fatna Rahhu's shepherd was! When I returned at night, I led the cattle into the barn, tied them fast, fed them, and generally helped the woman with them. All of the women said I was a splendid shepherd. She [Fatna Rahhu] asked me to stay with her. She promised me her daughter. "My house will be your house," she said. I told her I would do everything she wanted but that she must let me leave whenever I wanted to. I stayed a year and a half. When I got back to Meknes, I learned that my mother was dead.

What is most striking about this recitation is that, despite its attestation of independence, it has the autonomous quality of a dream. Tuhami is passive before the forces of fate. One is not quite sure whether the "someone" is man, demon, or saint. He takes care of Tuhami; he provides him not only with a job but with a mother and even a wife. He is father to Tuhami. Tuhami is immediately given extraordinary responsibility: the sole care of forty-five head of cattle! Tuhami's worth is recognized, by a

woman ("All of the women said I was a splendid shepherd").
The desire to be protected by a man and recognized and accepted by a woman is as strong here, if not stronger, than the
desire for independence and manhood.* A shepherd in
Morocco, and elsewhere in the Mediterranean, is often without a
family connection—he is an outsider, an orphan, too poor to
marry—and the ordinary standards of sexual behavior are not
applied to him. There is no romantic pastoral tradition here.
Rather, there are rumors—and the fact—of bestiality (Crapanzano 1977c). Mernissi (1975) quotes a letter from a young man
of the *bled:*

> "I fell in love with a girl in the village, and she was aware of it.
> I did not have money. . . . A civil servant came along and took
> away the girl I loved. So, I will not hide this from you, I went
> back to the animals again." [Mernissi 1975, p. 54]

On still another occasion Tuhami described what appears to
me to be the most likely sequence of events. (I cannot resist
finding "reality" in Tuhami's narrative!) His mother used to
bring him to work with her each morning and "then, when she
was old and tired"—no more than a year or two could have
passed—she asked Mme Jolan to give her son work.

— My mother was white. She worked for a Frenchwoman, the
woman where I was to work. I always used to go to work with my
mother. My mother always said I was not her son, because I was
black. Then, when she got older and tired, she told the French
lady that I was her son and asked her to give me work. . . .
— Why didn't your mother tell her you were her son?
— My mother liked me and was afraid that the Frenchwoman
would take me to France if she knew I was her son.

Tuhami's fantasy of his mother's fear, or perhaps his mother's
actual fear, of kidnapping was not uncommon. Fatima's fear had
little basis, of course, since Mme Jolan had established herself
permanently in Meknes. But poor Moroccans often feared that
their children would be carried off to France. More than a de-
cade after Independence, I still heard stories of child abductions

---

*The latter desire is given expression in Tuhami's refusal to marry Fatna's
daughter. His refusal—and his demand for independence—are reminiscent of
the stance one ought to take toward 'A'isha Qandisha and other *jinniyya*s.

and stories of mothers who voluntarily gave their sons, less frequently their daughters, to Frenchwomen to take home with them. Many of these stories were said to have occurred just after Independence. Tuhami explained that the Frenchwomen wanted the children "to work for them because they had no children of their own or because they just wanted to have dark-skinned people in their house." The stories reflect the Moroccan's ambivalence toward the French and, more generally, the colonized's ambivalence toward the colonizer.

The question remains, nevertheless: Why should Fatima's denial that Tuhami was her son prevent Mme Jolan from kidnapping him? Did her denial—or Tuhami's insistence on her denial—reflect a fear that working for the European involved a possession so complete that it extended even to a woman's son? Was Fatima's secret a way, for her, of maintaining autonomy? It was only when she was "older and tired" that she gave it up. Or was Fatima's fear of kidnapping really an expression of her desire to be rid of Tuhami? Or her ambivalence toward him? She always took Tuhami to work with her; she denied him her motherhood. Or did Tuhami's response reflect his own ambivalence? his desire to be kidnapped—possessed—by Mme Jolan? by a European? by me, his interlocutor? I posed the question—it was our first meeting—and Tuhami addressed me in his answer. We hardly knew each other; we were trying to establish a relationship. I was the European; I was a man. Did I offer, even then, the possibility of symbolic redemption?

• • •

— I continued working, and later, when I asked about my mother, I found out that she was dead. At that time I was working as a shepherd for a Berber. It was then that I found out she was dead.

A lot of people had been asking my mother why I was still living at home. They were bothering me with the same question. I left so as to be alone. I worked near El Hajeb. Then, when I came back to Meknes, I worked for the Frenchwoman again. The Berber brought me into town one day. He said, "Go and see your mother. I've marketing to do. In the evening we'll go back home." I went directly to Mme Jolan and learned that my mother was dead.* The Berber came, and Mme Jolan told him that my mother was dead and that she was keeping me.

— How did you feel when you learned that your mother had died?

— It meant nothing to me. (*He moved his hand downward in defiant dismissal.*) What good would it have done if I cried? Or hit my head against a wall? What could happen? Death is death.

— Were you sorry to leave?

— No! I could have done nothing. She wanted me to leave. Even if I had been there, I couldn't have stopped her from dying. It would have been worse. I would have cried. Thank God we have death. If there were no death, there would be as many people on earth as there are stars in the heavens.

Tuhami's attitude toward death is cold and fatalistic. The occasion of death is inevitable, unpredictable, impersonal, and autonomous. Moroccans of his background do not usually mark graves with the name of the dead; only the burialplaces of saints are remembered after time has passed. Death dates are commemorated no more than birth dates. The period of mourning is short—forty days, at most, for everyone but a widow, who must wear white for three months and ten days. (This period—a month less than the widow's mourning period prescribed by the Prophet—is to insure that a widow, before remarrying, knows whether or not she carries her dead husband's child.) The dead are quickly forgotten. Genealogies are shallow. Graves are rarely attended for very long. Cemeteries are visited on the New Year, the Feast of 'Ashur; water is sprinkled over the graves of friends and relatives "to cool the body," Tuhami says, "and to feed the soul [*ruh*]." Alms are given to the poor, and verses from the Koran are recited. What is done on 'Ashur is said to be efficacious throughout the coming year. Cemeteries are also visited on the twenty-seventh of Ramadan, the fearsome Night of Power, *lilt l-qadr*, when the *jnun*, imprisoned during the preceding days of the month, are released, and on other feast days as well. Of course, if one dreams of the dead, one should visit his or her grave and give alms to the poor, for the soul of the deceased is thought to have come to the dreamer to complain of his suffering and to ask relief through alms.

*Tuhami's mother died at the well as she was fetching water.

The vision of the afterlife is harsh and judgmental.* "The day when the Trumpet is blown...on that day we assemble the guilty, white-eyed (with terror)..." (Koran, sura 20, 1. 102, in Pickthall 1963). There is no belief in ghosts or other ancestral spirits who haunt the living. There is no worship of the ancestor. "Death starts in the big toe of the right foot," an old body-washer and pallbearer from Tuhami's neighborhood told me; and he continued:

"It feels like ants crawling under the skin. It climbs up the legs to the waist and then to the navel. When it reaches the navel, the dying man can talk but can no longer be heard. If he has been virtuous, he will tell his family to pay his debts before death reaches this point—and where to bury him and how much cloth to buy for his shroud. There are others—the wicked who hesitate to report their debts. Then it is too late. When death climbs above the navel, the dying can no longer be heard. When it reaches the lungs, the death rattle begins. Then you know it is all over. The soul [ruh] is in the throat. As the soul leaves the body, the mouth opens; sometimes it closes afterward. You should have water at the side of the dying at this time. When the mouth opens you dip a rag into the water and squeeze a few drops into the throat. It is said that death has pulled a chain along with it and scraped the throat of the dying. The water soothes it. This happens only to those who have eaten forbidden food, like pork.

"Death is announced by the angel of death, Sidina 'Azrain. It is sent by God. If a virtuous man dies, Sidina 'Azrain himself takes the soul. The soul goes to Barzakh, which looks like a beehive, where it remains until the Day of Judgment. It descends to the body on Fridays. Each hole in the hive belongs to someone; his name, according to his mother, is written on it. Youssef ben 'A'isha, for example. God said: People have left the earth; they will return to the earth and leave it yet again. When the world has been destroyed, God will ask Sidina 'Azrain to look around to see if anyone yet lives. God will then tell Sidina 'Azrain to put his own soul in the hive. He alone among

*Contrast with LeTourneau (1949; 1965) and Hart (1976). The Moroccans in Tuhami's milieu stress both the contingency of death and the final judgment made thereafter. LeTourneau's observation that the cemeteries in Fez are freely visited by casual strollers applies also to the cemeteries in Meknes. Although the *jnun*, as Tuhami maintains, often gravitate to cemeteries, they are not usually feared there.

the angels has a hole. When he dies, sperm will rain on the earth. The dead will grow from the earth up to their navels and remain stuck this way until another angel, Sidina 'Israfil, sneezes. It is Sidina 'Israfil who announces the Day of Judgment with his trumpet. When the angel sneezes, then the dead will sneeze and say praise to God and be released from the earth. They will have stiff bodies which cannot bend down and eyes on top of their heads; for otherwise they would see one another in their nakedness.

"Now begins the reckoning. Each human being has two angels on his shoulders. The angel on the right shoulder keeps track of good deeds; the angel on the left shoulder keeps track of bad deeds. These angels bring their lists to an angel who keeps count like a notary. First the angel on the right reports the good deeds; then the angel on the left the bad deeds. The good deeds are placed in one cup, the bad in another. Each person must carry the two cups across a bridge that is finer than a hair and sharper than a razor to a scale where they are balanced one against the other. The bridge crosses the fires of Hell. The righteous cross the bridge like lightning; the wicked stumble across it, losing their balance and cutting themselves. Those who have more good deeds will go to Paradise; those who have more bad deeds will go to Hell.

"When everyone's deeds have been weighed, there are only two names: Sa'id and Shaqi. Sa'id is the name of the good, and Shaqi is the name of the wicked. It is very hot. There are seven heavens. The sun is usually in the seventh heaven, but not at this time. It is in the first heaven. Everyone is burning. Birds of Paradise drip water from the River Kutar [al-Kawthar] on their parents. (The river flows from under God's throne.) These birds of Paradise are the children who died before they could talk. Their souls were brought by angels called nomadic camels [jmal rehhala] directly to the Prophet's daughter, Lalla Fatima Zahara, in Paradise. Lalla Fatima Zahara takes care of them.

"The houris lead those with the name Sa'id to Paradise. There are seven levels of Paradise. Where you go depends on your good deeds. There are seven levels of Hell, too. The uzbaniyat [the zabaniya, literally, the "violent thrusters," the guards of hell] lead those called Shaqi there. Christians, Jews, and pagans are in the lowest level. There are Muslims there, too. Sidina Mohammed looks through the seven levels of Hell. "I want my people all to go to Paradise," he says. God agrees.

The Christians want their Prophet to intercede for them, but he can't. He asks only for himself. The Jews want Sidina Musa [Moses] to get them into Paradise. He says that he is not sure if he himself can get in, let alone all the other Jews.

"The Muslims smell in Hell. This smell is unbearable to even those in the lowest level of Paradise. They must bathe in the River Kutar before they can enter Paradise. The houris lead them in. Finally only the Muslims who have hit their parents are left in Hell. Their parents must excuse them. They refuse. 'We worked for our children,' they say. 'And they hit us; they abandoned us. We do not forgive them.' It is only when Sidina Mohammed promises to raise them to a higher level of Paradise that they forgive their children."

Tuhami shared the body-washer's vision of death and the afterlife, although he never presented his vision in as complete and coherent a fashion. The vision is, of course, a corruption of Koranic and traditional eschatology. Tuhami emphasized the punishments in Hell, particularly for sexual offenses. A homosexual, he told me, will receive a hundred blows. He will be suspended by his eyelids below the anus of the man with whom he has had intercourse. His own sperm will drip into his open mouth. His partner will also be suspended by his eyelids. Onanists and men who have not paid the prostitutes they slept with will suffer similar punishments. A man who has not said his prayers in life must repeat them after death in a well filled with snakes and scorpions, which will bite him each time he tries to escape. If he does escape, he will be condemned to say his prayers on a board so hot that it will scorch the skin from his forehead.

Tuhami claimed Koranic authority for such punishments. He did not dwell on them morbidly. They reflect his sexual puritanism and his generally pessimistic attitude toward life. "When you are happy," he said, "you know that someday you will be sad; therefore, you can never be completely happy."

•   •   •

"When I was little, I just ate and drank and played. I was not even sent to the mosque school." Tuhami said this with regret. He was ashamed not to be able to write even his name. He was sorry that his father had not seen fit to send him to the local mosque school. There he would have learned the alphabet and the Koran, or at any rate verses from the Koran, by heart— learned them without much comprehension from a teacher, a *fqih,* who was probably more interested in writing magic formulas for his clients than in giving instruction to the boys in his charge (see Eikelman 1978). Tuhami would at least have had some knowledge of the written word, and the written word was, for him, charged with mystery and power. He might even have become a man of learning. His ignorance kept him down; it prevented him even from marrying. "If I were to ask a virgin to marry me, she would say, 'I want someone civilized.' If I were to ask an older woman, she would say she wanted a civil servant."

Tuhami played, instead, at the river's edge with other boys. He tried to catch a glimpse of the little girls who came to the river to bathe. He joked, foolishly, about the *jnun* who lived at the bottom of the river. He caught birds, tied long strings to their legs, let them fly off, and pulled them back again and again until they died of exhaustion. He learned dimly about the sex play of older boys: mutual masturbation and anal intercourse (usually without penetration). He knew, too, that shepherd boys often played with their sheep and goats. He left the countryside before he was ready for such play. He guarded his father's sheep for only a few months before his departure for Meknes. He witnessed the death of a friend, whose name, like the name of his stepfather, he never told me.

Tuhami could not recall much else about his earliest childhood, not even the birth of his brother, 'Ali, or his sister, Rakya. They were three or four years younger than he was. He did not remember the affection his mother showed him. He slept on a little straw mattress next to her and Driss. She gave him her breast whenever he cried (I am reconstructing here from traditional Moroccan child-rearing practices)—that is, until he was about two. Then Khadija, his grandmother, the midwife, told her it was time to wean him. Perhaps, then, she would conceive again. There was no infant in her belly who would poison her milk out of jealousy for Tuhami. Fatima smeared a red-pepper paste on her breast and showed it to her son. "See what you have done," she said. "Your teeth are too sharp." Tuhami cried. He had felt the gnawing pain in his gums. His mother had rubbed them; she had given him a knotted rag to chew. She had pushed him away angrily when he nibbled at her nipples. And now, even when he cried, she did not give him her breast. "Crying is not good for men or women," Tuhami told me once. "It is worse for me to cry."

Tuhami did not remember playing with his father. Driss did not hit him much, though; he was not like some of the other fathers in the village, who tied up their sons for a beating so that they would not flinch or struggle. Tuhami learned from the neighborhood boys and girls not to pee or soil his pants. His mother and grandmother knew that he would learn when he was ready.

Tuhami did not remember his circumcision. Some Moroccan men do. He was perhaps too young. It took place in the country, before he moved to Meknes. He could not yet count. "I learned to count when I was five," he said once, without real regard for chronology.

The circumcision was obviously painful. Here again I am reconstructing on the basis of both subjective accounts I heard of the circumcision ritual and my observations of it (Crapanzano 1980). Tuhami was dressed in his best clothes—a new white *jallaba* His mother had bathed him carefully. He was put on a horse and led through the village, at the head of a dusty procession, to the red-clay ruins that served as a mosque. A little whitewash had been splashed around the entrance years before. No muezzin had ever called prayers from it. Tuhami was made to circumambulate the mosque three times and then enter it to say a prayer. Of course he knew no prayers and listened, a little in awe, a little afraid, to an old man in his father's family mumble the few holy words he happened to know. He was returned, again on horseback, to the house, where preparations for a feast were under way. It was just after the harvest; there was a lot to eat—couscous, *tajin* with olives and lemon, freshly baked bread with thick brown crusts. A sheep had been sacrificed earlier in the morning. It had been oriented toward Mecca, and his grandfather had muttered the appropriate ritual formula before he slit its throat. Tuhami had seen the thick red blood flow slowly from its neck. The earth was still stained purple.

Tuhami was the center of attention. It was his day. He had no idea what was going to happen (as Moroccans who remembered

their own circumcisions stereotypically reported to me). Of
course, there had been circumcisions in the village before, and
Tuhami had been taken to them.

His father disappeared. His mother led him through the
crowd of relatives, friends, neighbors, and perhaps even a few
men whom his father and grandfather did not like much; past
the young girls, still virgin, who had let down their long black
hair (a circumcision was the only time they could ever do this in
public), past the strangers who had come that morning. The
strangers, who were musicians, had taken out their *ghita*s, belled
oboes made of apricot wood, and were moistening the double
reeds. The women with them—one woman, at least, performed
with the musicians—were walking around freely, smiling and
talking to the village men as no village woman would ever do.
They wore bright colors and silver and gold brocaded belts,
buckled tightly just below their breasts.

Tuhami's mother handed him over to an older man he hardly
knew. He was led into a small room; a blanket was pulled across
the door. The crowd outside gathered around it. Tuhami's
mother, Fatima, took off her slippers. She put her left foot in a
bowl of cold water with a piece of iron at the bottom; this was to
cool the pain of circumcision. With her left hand she held a
mirror to her face; this was to quell the tears of pain. With her
right hand she held up a white banner, the mark of Islam.

Tuhami could not see his mother, outside the door. The old
man held him, pulling his legs apart. A stranger—the barber—
who had arrived that morning with the musicians and the whore
dancers, knelt before him, sharpening his scissors. Tuhami's
chemise was pulled up to his navel. He was told to look up at the
birds. The barber deftly put a bit of manure between Tuhami's
glans—the head, he called it—and his foreskin and with a single
movement cut off the foreskin. He plunged the bleeding penis
into a cracked egg to which he had added rabbit droppings. This
was to cool the penis and encourage healing. A signal was given.
The musicians began to play the loud whining songs of the circumcision ceremony.

Tuhami could feel nothing. He did not look down. He was
afraid his penis had been cut off. He was lifted up, placed on his
mother's back, and wrapped tightly in a blanket. Warmth is said
to heal the wound. His mother began to dance. He felt her body

undulate, and her salty perspiration trickled down her back and stung his penis. She had arranged her clothes in such a way that his penis, pushed against her naked back, would not stain her festival clothes with blood. When she stopped dancing, the whore dancers began to belly-dance. The villagers watched them, the women critically and the men salaciously. Tuhami was left in a corner, desolate, whimpering to himself. A little sack containing harmal and *shiba* (absinthe) was tied to his right leg to protect him from the evil eye. He was particularly vulnerable to the evil eye now. He was not so weak, though, as to have a woman's necklace made of a lark's skull, a camel's bone, and a piece of amber placed over his right shoulder. The next day, life would be back to normal for Tuhami, but he would still avoid looking at his penis, for fear that it was gone, and he would dread the burning pain when he urinated.

Circumcision is said to make a man and a Muslim of a boy. It gives tone, emotional cathexis, to the experience of life—to sex, manhood, one's mother and father, and, of course, to the figure of the stranger, the barber, who, according to Tuhami, possesses great magic and the knowledge of many cures.* In Morocco, circumcision is a precocious ritual (Crapanzano 1980). It has been called a rite of passage, marking the change of status from boy to man, but I am not convinced that there is in fact any passage. Disjunction between the *real* and the *symbolic*, the natural and the cultural, may in fact be its point. The little boy, seldom more than four, is symbolically declared a man before he is in any sense a man. He leaves the women's world for a moment, only to return to it scarred. His desires—and the Freudians would have much to say about the oedipal implications of this—are stymied. His manhood is declared by the act of mutilating—destroying—the very proof of his manhood. (Boys are sometimes told that they will undergo a second circumcision if they are not good.) Moroccan men often joke about circumcision, especially in the baths. They talk of the mutilated and those with jagged foreskins and those—they are actually very rare—who have lost their penises. There is much anxiety. The lines

*Barbers traditionally performed simple operations; today they still act as bleeders, drawing blood from people whose blood is "heavy" and who tire easily and suffer from the summer heat. They also shave the head of the groom at an important prenuptial ceremony.

between manhood and womanhood, that great social-symbolic cleavage in the Arab world, is not very clear after all. To be symbolically a man, one must be rendered as really as possible a woman. To be really a man, one must be rendered as symbolically as possible a woman. Resolution is sought in the ritual instant. But as Sartre (1964) observes, the instant is "the reciprocal and contradictory envelopment of the before by the after." The Moroccan man lives through time outliving the ritual instant that declared him to be what he is not and not to be what he is. Definitions, whether of self or other, are always dialectical. Ritual attempts to fix them, but life—the *real*, the natural—belies ritual. And so rituals must be reproduced in life and words. It is perhaps our longing for the fixed, the real collapsed into the symbolic, nature collapsed into ritual, that has led us in the West to see such rites as rites of passage, rites of smooth and continuous transition from one state to another, rather than as violent rites of disjunction that are in essence, and perhaps in function, purposefully disjunctive.

•   •   •

Fatima's death completed Tuhami's abandonment. He was thrust into the hands of the woman who his mother feared would abduct him. He was cast into the alien world of the *colon*—to be protected and exploited. He became a victim of the *colon*'s ambivalence. For a time he sought security in his maternal grandfather, Moulay 'Abdeslem, the man whose name he took as his patronymic; but Moulay 'Abdeslem was old and soon died .

— Mme Jolan saw me crying. She brought me to her house. My brother and sister had already been taken to Casablanca to live with my mother's sister. I looked all around the *medina* for my mother's father. He had rented a room there. I found him cooking a stew. He was happy there all by himself. He told me we would go to Casablanca in a month to see my brother and sister.

Tuhami worked as a porter at the Jolan factory and moved in with Moulay 'Abdeslem, "who was 160 years old and could still walk all the way to Sidi 'Ali's tomb."

— He didn't talk about anything besides the war. He had fought with 'Abdel Krim in the Rif. He told me about his marriage. He had taken his wife by force, and for twenty-two days all he did was to fight off her other suitors. "I found her all alone," he told me. "All the men wanted to marry her. One man in particular tried to take her away from me, but she killed him. She told me she wanted to put an end to the story. She hugged him and then stabbed him in the heart." My grandfather told me she was very brave. She could use a rifle. After she killed the man, she told my grandfather. He jumped up. "What you have done to that man," he said "you will do to me." Then the two of them decided to leave. They came to a bridge. There were some thieves there. They wanted her. They were on the opposite side of the river. They fought my grandfather for five days. Then, after several of them were killed, the thieves fled. The girl picked up a rifle and aimed it at my grandfather and told him she'd shoot him if he didn't marry her. He said he would, and he did.

Such tales of the powers of women, particularly Berber women, are not uncommon. Women in the Middle Atlas mountains, Jean d'Esme reports, were not to be outdone by men in combat: "Although they were under the fire of our machine guns, women crawled with extraordinary courage to the water holes. The majority were killed, but the survivors carried on, nonetheless, the heroic task of provisioning" (Brignon et al. 1967). Sometimes they actually fought. They aroused the men with "strident ululations, distributed ammunition, took the place of the dying, and rolled enormous stones down onto their assailants, spreading death to the end of the wadi" (ibid.). The "snuff" fantasy, apparently common enough in the West, is not unknown in Morocco.

When Moulay 'Abdeslem had saved enough money for the trip, he took Tuhami to Casablanca.

— We went by train. It was the first time I had ever been on a train. I thought I was the most important person in the world. In the morning we found ourselves in Casablanca. We found the right street, but my grandfather couldn't remember the house number. I knocked on every door on the street. They kept telling me to try the neighbors. I knocked at the fourth house, and it was my Aunt Hadda! She began to cry. I told her not to cry. "It is finished. It is all in the past," I said. We spent two months in Casablanca, and then we took the train back to Meknes. It was the month of Ramadan.

It was while Tuhami was in Casablanca that he learned, from his sister, about his mother's concern for him. She had looked all over Meknes for him. She consulted the scribes (*tolba*), who give advice, occasionally practice divination, and write magical formulas, and she went to seers almost every day. They were of no help. She never did learn where he was.

— After Ramadan my grandfather and I went to work for Mme Jolan. Then he married again and went to work in the tile factory across from Mme Jolan's—the one where I work now, the one owned by the Moroccan. Mme Jolan told me not to live with him. She gave me a room in her place. I stayed there until my grandfather divorced his wife. Then I went to live with him again. He didn't want me. "It's because of you," he said, "that I had to get divorced. You were always coming around for food, for bread, to have your clothes washed."

Mme Jolan did not like Moulay 'Abdeslem very much. He had lived at her factory for a while, but he had left when he took sick and Mme Jolan had ordered him to see a doctor. It was at about this time that he had married again. Tuhami continued:

— So I went to work at the other factory. I worked there at night for a month. One night someone called me: "Tuhami!" I turned around, and a rock hit my knee. I fell down on the spot. I was sick for three months. I went to the scribes [who are thought to have curative powers], but they couldn't help. One night, after the month of Ramadan, my grandfather was preparing shish kebab for me because I was still sick. Our room caught on fire. Some one told Mme Jolan, and she ran right over. She saved us from burning to death. A man—his name was Sidi Mohammed—helped me drag my grandfather out of the fire. He was completely burned. Mme Jolan took my grandfather's head in her lap and told him to repeat the profession of faith because he was dying. He said, "Thank you. Don't abandon

Tuhami. He is sick. He has something in his bones ['*adam*]."* Mme Jolan promised that she would take care of me as if I were her son. The ambulance came to get my grandfather, but by the time it arrived he was dead. Mme Jolan and her daughter, Annette, took me to their house.

Tuhami was very calm as he described the death of his grandfather. In an earlier version, in which he was not supported by Mme Jolan, he described his feelings in what I must take to be a more realistic fashion. I had asked him if he had ever lost consciousness.

— Only once, after my grandfather died. He was the last of my family. I was all alone, with just my sister. [Rakya was in Casablanca at the time, and his brother 'Ali was in Sidi Rahal, where he worked for the provincial secretary.] I did not know what to do. I did not know where to go. Where to work. Where to eat. The boss of the factory where I worked told me to stay there at the factory. I spent the night, and in the morning I asked myself what I could eat. I didn't even know. The boss came up to me and asked me what I was doing. "Why aren't you working?" he asked. I started to work, but I couldn't work like the others. The other workers boycotted me because I couldn't work like them. I decided to remain just to earn enough to survive on until I could find another job.

Then I went to work on a farm near Rabat. A forester lived nearby. There was a German steward on the farm. One day he drove past the factory; he saw me and asked me what I was doing. I told him, and he asked if I wanted to work for him. I said I did. He said that I'd have to come immediately. I told him I couldn't, and he answered that then he couldn't hire me. I agreed to come right away. He went into town to do some errands, and I went to tell my boss. I told him I wanted to take a trip. (*Tuhami seemed to take pride in misleading his boss.*) When the steward came back, I got into his car. After a while he said that I was not going to work with the other workers but to carry water out to them. When we got to the farm, the foreman—his name

*Symbolic for the fact that he is troubled by the *jnun*. '*Adam* may be used for epilepsy and other seizures (Mercier 1951). Epilepsy is explained in terms of the *jnun*. See below, p. 159.

was Ahmed—saw me and said, "My God, why did you bring him?" He knew me because I had worked on the farm before.

Tuhami was becoming confused. He explained that the foreman had made the comment because he was black. It is likely, though, that Tuhami had worked on the farm before. Many workers leave Meknes at harvest time to work on nearby farms. But a water carrier is, like a shepherd, an outsider.

— The first day I was on the farm I was paid without having to work. The next day I was given two barrels, a cart, and a mule. I went to the field, and the workers, who knew me from before, asked me what I was doing there. I said, "I used to work here; I left; and now I'm back." I worked as a water carrier for two months. Then I worked in the house for another month.

The steward had two wives, a French one and a Berber one. He told me, "If your work does not satisfy the women, I'll send you to Rabat [to the government authorities]." (*Tuhami laughed as he repeated the steward's words.*)

My work was good, and I could eat with the women. One day I ate with one of them, the next with the other. The Berber had a daughter who told the steward that her mother was feeding me. I didn't know this. One day he came up to me. "Listen Tuhami," he said, "tell me the truth, I'll give you a raise if you tell me the truth, and you'll be able to eat in my house. Have you been eating in my house already?" "If I'm to answer you," I said, "you must tell me who told you." He said it was the cook. Then I told him that I could not answer because there would be trouble. He said, "Come with me. We'll eat in the house. We'll eat with Anne-Marie. Have you ever talked to her?" I answered that I had only said good morning. Inside, he asked the Frenchwoman something which I couldn't understand. But I think it was the same question he had asked me. He watched us all through the meal to see whether we signaled each other with our eyes. (*Tuhami laughed strangely. He was very nervous.*) Then, after dinner, I excused myself. The steward told me not to go back to work. He ordered me to take a walk with both women. I asked the cook, later, if he had told the steward anything. He said he hadn't, and we became friends. After that I left.

Tuhami's story ran out. He seemed emotionally drained. "My grandfather helped me." Tuhami, his history over, began to elaborate. "He encouraged me; he gave me the force to work. When he died, I could no longer work." In this recitation, there was no happy interlude with the Jolans between the death of the last member of his family and the period of severe depression that he characterized as "the time I slept in the cemeteries." (In a later interview, Tuhami placed his work on the farm in this period of depression.) He never again mentioned the episode with the German steward's wives. His recitation—real or fantasied—could not sustain him.

·   ·   ·

— Mme Jolan gave me turkey eggs, for strength, and injections. She gave them to me herself. I kept getting worse. I told her it wasn't working, and I asked her to take me to the hospital.* Everyone in the family began to cry. Mme Jolan said that I should be taken to the hospital. . . . I was put into a room with three beds. Mme Jolan told the people in the hospital that she would pay for everything and that they should let her family visit me. I spent seven months there. There were day and night nurses. The night nurse came and gave me some medicine. She began to talk to me. What I heard tickled my ear. She told me about Sidina Musa [Moses] and Sidina 'Isa [Jesus]. She was Spanish; the day nurse was French. Her name was Michèle.

I used to eat three eggs and a pint of milk each day. They tried all kinds of medicine, but none of them worked. One day a military doctor came. He told me I had been there a long time. He smiled and said, very slowly, "You will get better! You have three months. You will get better in that time, whether with the grace of God or without the grace of God." I thanked him. He changed my nurses. He said, "I'll give all of the money Mme Jolan has paid for your care to you when you leave. You will have a big feast [sadaqa] with it. You have been sick for a long time. Others have come and gone. You are a marabout [a saint].

At five each day the nurse gave me a shower. Then she would take me for a walk in the hospital garden. I would feel better. Then she gave me a cup of black coffee and two eggs, one cooked and one raw. I ate both of them. I would then begin to

---

*The hospital to which Tuhami refers was a general medical facility and not a psychiatric installation.

perspire. For two months I did this. By the third month I could go outside and run around. The doctor was satisfied. "Now is the time for the celebration," he said. I told him that I had nothing to pay him; "God alone must thank you," I said. He told me to pray for him. I wanted to leave, but the doctor told me to stay for the rest of the month. Then they let Mme Jolan know I was leaving. All my friends thought that I was dying and that they were so sick of me at the hospital that they were sending me home. The doctor rented a buggy for me, and I arrived at Mme Jolan's. You would have thought I was about to be married. Mme Jolan and all her daughters and her sister were there next to me. Mme Jolan said I had four months to do whatever I wanted and that I would be paid for it. It was at this time that Mme Jolan's son Jean-Pierre was dissatisfied. I went all over with the Jolan children. Mme Jolan's son thought I must be her true son—and that he was not. People began to whisper that I was making love to Mme Jolan. One might I went for a walk and did not return. I slept everywhere at that time—in the cemeteries. That is my life's story.

Tuhami's "illness" was most probably a condensation of several different illnesses, for on a number of occasions his reports of it were contradictory, like his reports of the events that occurred after his father's death. (The "someone" who called him was a *jinn*—abstract here, impersonal, without gender or personality— a *jinn* who was to be metamorphosed again and again into more concrete shapes in the recitation of his life.) Whatever the cause of the illness, if in fact it occurred as Tuhami described it, it served—or at least serves here, in the recitation—to fix his relations with the Jolan family. The Jolans took him in, cared for him, sent him to the hospital, where he was mothered by the nurses, who told stories that tickled his ears, and fathered by the doctor, who took command of the situation. Notice the emphasis Tuhami gives to the doctor's suggestions. He was particularly susceptible to suggestion. Traditional Moroccan cures operate not through confession but through suggestion and definition.

Tuhami returned from the hospital in a buggy. He was the center of attention. Significantly, he said: "You would have thought I was about to be married." He was the center of the women's world—but not like the circumcised boy who returns to that world only to be ignored: "Mme Jolan and all her daughters and her sister were there next to me." He became one of the family: "I went all over with the Jolan children." But the Paradise had to end. Tuhami was dark-skinned, Moroccan, a Muslim. Mme Jolan set a time limit on her indulgence. Jean-Pierre was less patient.* Tuhami was hostile to him, the son-brother, but not to M. Jolan, who remained as nameless as his stepfather. In Morocco the elder brother bears the hostility to the father (see Ortigues and Ortigues 1966, for Senegal).

"Mme Jolan's son thought I must be the true son—and that he was not": This theme is common in fairytales. (Its observation may be psychologically accurate too.) The beggar-orphan is the true son of the queen; the prince is the bastard. Tuhami expresses a wish in terms of the Other's fantasy. The fantasies of the Other, even when we ourselves invent them, are always more real than those we attribute to ourselves.

The Other, more impersonal here than Jean-Pierre, mediates reality: "People began to whisper that I was making love to Mme Jolan." (This recitation is late; Tuhami could not have admitted the rumor earlier.) Desire is expressed through rumor, through the Other's fantasy. Tuhami had to flee, to the cemetery. The rumor, if not indicative of the *real*, was perhaps too close to his true desire. His life ended for him then—aspiration, hope, sexual conquest, family, warmth, mothering and fathering, the possibility of wealth, marriage, and children. The rest of his story is the story of his being as dead.

• • •

— Mme Jolan's son said there was something going on between his mother and me.

— What did he mean?

— He thought that Mme Jolan was going to give me one of her daughters to marry. Mme Jolan had given them all Muslim

---

*Tuhami told me on another occasion that Jean-Pierre was always friendly to him, spoke Arabic and Berber, and taught him to cut tiles.

names.* They knew how to cook Moroccan food. I left at that time. (*Tuhami stopped.*)

— Did you ever kiss any of her daughters?

— No. (*Tuhami was very embarrassed.*)

— Did you ever want to?

— The girls wanted to, but I didn't. I used to take them all over. Once Mme Jolan's sister came to visit. Her name was Sylvie. She had two girls. Both of them were sick. She asked the workers in the factory to pray for them. She promised to give a feast [*sadaqa*] if the girls got better. When Sylvie arrived, Mme Jolan told me to stay around after dinner. I was surrounded by women and spent the evening telling them stories. Then M. Jolan came in and asked what was going on. I got up to leave, but Mme Jolan told me to stay. She brought over a table and asked me to beat out the rhythm of a German parade march. I did, and they all laughed. Then they asked me to tell them about Charlie Chaplin. I talked and talked until everyone had fallen asleep. I covered them up and sat down and watched them until morning.

In the morning M. Jolan said, "So that is what you wanted." I answered that it wasn't I who wanted it but his wife. Mme Jolan bought me new clothes that day, and I didn't have to work for a month but was paid anyway.

In a month Sylvie's two girls were cured. Sylvie's husband came for the feast. He wanted to take me back to Algeria, where they lived. I had been helping Sylvie and her two daughters for three months. She had praised me to her husband. I agreed to go with them, but Mme Jolan didn't want me to. They said to me, "We'll meet you at the station." When they were leaving, Mme Jolan watched from the roof to make sure I didn't go. Then she went down to the factory and asked where I was. They said I wasn't there. Mme Jolan came after me in a buggy (*Tuhami imitated a horse clownishly*), and she caught me at the station. "So you want to go to Algeria," she said. "You must never change the old for the new." She brought me back with her and insulted her sister.

_____

*In fact, the Jolan girls did not have Muslim names; they may have had Muslim nicknames, but this seems unlikely.

Tradition—in the guise of protection—must be preserved as long as (and inasmuch as) it facilitates exploitation. Of course, the *colon* would never admit to so crude a statement of motivation. The protection he provides also provides him with a source of rationalization, justification, and sentiment. The rationalizations and justifications are believed; the sentiments are heartfelt. If we are to believe Tuhami, Mme Jolan was genuinely attached to him. She took him into her family; he played with the children, ate with them, went to the movies with them, and, for a time, slept in the same house with them. But, unlike her children, he was never sent to school—was never even taught French. He was subject to Mme Jolan's caprice. One day he worked in the tile factory, where his work—carrying clay tiles into and out of the kiln—was grueling and dangerous to his health. The next day he served as a houseboy. Another day he could play with the children and still receive his pay. Tuhami accommodated himself to the situation as long as he could and as best he could. He became a clown and a storyteller.

Both clown and storyteller achieve their identity by exploiting, often without awareness, the ambiguities of their culture and the ambivalence of their social position. Tuhami often did not know what he was doing. Much of the amusement he inspired resulted precisely from his ignorance of the *moeurs*—and the language—of the Jolan family. He certainly did not understand the significance of a German parade march of the 1930s. And he certainly did not understand the relationship between the sexes that prevailed among *colons*. "I was surrounded by women. . . . Then M. Jolan came in and asked what was going on. I got up to leave." One can see the frightened boy jump up as the father enters and asks, perhaps crossly, what is going on. Tuhami was, in his, in traditional, terms, in a forbidden paradise: alone, the center of attention, with half a dozen women, some of them virgins, or presumably so, and others attached to men.

With genius, Tuhami was able to recreate this scene again and again in his later life. He has sat alone among women in traditional Moroccan households! His gift for storytelling and his clowning has enabled him to achieve this anomalous position in his own society, just as they had in the Jolan household. It was a position not without cost, for Tuhami surrendered his real manhood in order to achieve what, I must presume, was a symbolic conquest. His tales were, as I have said, seductions.

— Did Mme Jolan want to make love to you?
— Yes. Both she and her sister wanted to make love to me. (*Tuhami was very embarrassed.*) Once I was in prison. There was a lieutenant who lived nearby with his wife. He thought that I had made love to his wife. One day a car came for me and took me to the lieutenant's. "Tell me the truth," he said, "or I'll bash your head in." I answered that I preferred my head bashed in. He then sent me to the police station. The chief called me in and told the others to get out. "Sit down," he said, and offered me a cigarette. I told him I didn't smoke. He asked me if I drank, and I told him I didn't. "People have been saying things about you. Are they true?" he asked. I said, "No. If they were true do you think I would be dressed like this? I'd be better off." "Why not tell me the truth?" he asked. "I'll let you go anyway." I told him the things people were saying were lies. Then he called in the wife and asked her something. I couldn't understand, but I think she answered the same way I did. They let me go and made the lieutenant pay me five dirhams for the two days of work I had lost.

When I got back, Mme Jolan asked me where I had been. I said I hadn't been anywhere. She said, "I know where you were. *Tant pis.* I want to save you." Then I knew Mme Jolan wanted something. "Why do you want me to go to jail?" I asked. "I want it! I want it! I want it!" she screamed and slapped me. (*Tuhami laughed.*)

Her son was very happy then, but I told him she would pay for the slap within three days. One day, as we were waiting in line in front of her desk, she asked me to come around to the other side of her desk, but I refused. Then she told me not to be afraid, that she had only slapped me because we were in front of her son. She told me to be careful with her daughters. "If anything happens to them," she said, "there is only one man I know and that is you."

That night, after she slapped me, I went to the movies with the girls, and we stayed out until one o'clock. After the movies I said we should go back by taxi, but the girls wanted to walk. It was very dark, and every time we passed a tree, they were afraid someone was hiding behind it. I pressed them on. When we got back, I found Mme Jolan was still up. When I got to my room, I found new clothes and a new blanket. "What is going on?" I asked myself. "There is a big difference. I'm a little afraid." In the morning Mme Jolan told me that she trusted me. "I have a lot of money in the bank," she told me. "If I weren't afraid of losing it, I would change my nationality and become a Muslim." I answered, "I'm with you. I work for you. I consider you my relative. If you want anything else from me, I prefer to leave now." Mme Jolan hugged me. "Excuse me," she said, "I've chased after you a lot and I've always seen your eyes lowered. I know I've been wrong." I worked for her until her youngest daughter married, and then I said good-bye. There was a man from Meknes who saw her once in France. She asked about me, but he said he didn't know anything about me. Muslims don't want others to get ahead of them.

Tuhami assured me that he had never slept with the lieutenant's wife. "Why would I? It was the time of the French. If you were caught, it was your head. They have their own laws [*qanun*]." He never said that he had slept with Mme Jolan and never said that he had not slept with her. And there was something in his manner, in the discretion he demanded, that precluded either my asking him directly or Lhacen's asking him. (Lhacen was sure that he had slept with her once—on the night he returned from the movies and found the new clothes and the blanket.) The ending of his story—"I worked for her until her last daughter married, and then I said good-bye"—must be taken figuratively as a closure.

• • •

I asked Tuhami to tell me about his first experience with a woman. He said he was sixteen; the girl was a Berber. He was working for Mme Jolan.

— Mme Jolan had taken a three months' holiday in Casablanca. She took me with her. One day she sent me to the market on some errands. I saw a Berber woman at the gate. I winked, and she nodded. (*Tuhami indicated his surprise with a gesture.*)

She told me to hurry and do my errands and come back. "You'll wait?" I asked. "Yes," she answered, "if you hurry." I ran back to Mme Jolan's as fast as I could. She asked me what was wrong. I said nothing was wrong and ran back to the market. The Berber woman was still there. I asked her where we could go, and she said to come back to her house. Then she asked me whether I wanted to make love quickly or stay with her all day. "That depends on you," I said. "How much do you want?" "You don't have to pay," she answered; "I'm married. My husband is in the army. He's away all the time." "Do you do this sort of thing a lot?" I asked. "No, this is the first time." "Why did you nod in agreement when I winked?" I asked her. "I knew you were a stranger," she answered. "I knew there would be no problems." Then she asked me if I knew what to do. I said I didn't. "You have to take off your clothes," she explained. "Why?" I asked. "Do you think I was in an accident?" "No," she answered; "just take off your clothes." I did. Then she brought food and told me to stay all day and all night. "Who will tell Mme Jolan?" I asked. "If I stay, I'll lose my job." "I'll tell her," she answered. I said, "I'll stay until nightfall, and then you will have to ask Mme Jolan and ask her to let me spend the night." I stayed until six-thirty, and then we left for Mme Jolan's. I told her to go in front of me. When Mme Jolan saw us, she scratched her chin and told us to go back. I spent the night and returned the next morning.

— Did you ever see the Berber woman again?

— No. How could I? I never went back to Casablanca. It was too expensive.

— Did you enjoy it?

— Very much.

Tuhami grinned boyishly. He had laughed and exaggerated throughout his tale. He had in fact been coy, and he knew it. I imagined that he had entertained the Jolan family in the same tone. I found his lighthearted humor markedly different from the heaviness with which he had spoken, a few minutes earlier, of Mme Jolan's attempted seduction. Her persona here was much more lively. Of course, his statement that the Berber woman agreed to ask Mme Jolan's permission was totally preposterous. No Moroccan woman would ever agree to that kind of request. But for a moment Tuhami had caught the gaiety that was usually so painfully absent from his vision of the sexual relations between men and women.

"Once there was a Spanish girl I saw at the movies," Tuhami continued, almost immediately. I had asked him if Mme Jolan knew what he had been up to. He said that she did and that she had teased him about it afterwards.

— I was at the movies with Jean-Pierre. He pointed out the girl and said "O la la." I asked him what was the matter. "Look at that girl," he said. I looked and saw she was a Spanish girl I knew. I said, "She's nothing." Then he said, "Look. Let's see who can get her. If you get her, I'll pay for the movies. If I get her, you'll have to pay. But don't tell my mother." I agreed. We stood apart. The girl came by with an officer. I tripped her slightly. She said, "Careful." I said, "I didn't do it—not me." We talked for a while, and I asked whom she was with." She rubbed her finger to indicate that he was someone she wanted to marry. I said, "He's nothing. He's in the army. Don't marry him. He'll never be home. You should marry someone who will be home." "Do you know anyone?" she asked. "Me," I answered. Then Jean-Pierre came up to us and began to speak to her in Spanish. After the movies, he suggested we all go together for a snack. He said he couldn't treat but that I could. "You've got money. I'm broke. You work." I took them all to the cantina. There the Spanish girl touched my foot and smiled and told me to come to see her someday.

Afterward, Jean-Pierre was very angry. He couldn't work any more. He just stood in front of the Spanish girl's house. When Mme Jolan noticed this, she asked me what was the matter with him. I told her and offered to go with her if she wanted to arrange a marriage. "You're crazy," she answered. Then one day, Mme Jolan and I went to the Spaniard's house. Her father greeted us, and we all went inside. Mme Jolan asked the Spanish girl whom she had met first, her son or me. She said she had known me first. Then she invited them all to her house. It was a Sunday. She had a big couscous—chicken and rabbit. "Now we are in agreement," she said at one point. I thought it was a marriage feast. I jumped up and cried, "I'm not going to marry her. It's not for me." I pulled the girl and Jean-Pierre up and made them hold hands. Everyone laughed. Finally, Jean-Pierre married her. They had three children, and then she died.

The lighthearted moment could not be sustained. Tuhami's story was absurd and confused. He tried to exploit the confusion to convert it into entertainment, clownishness, a good tale. He failed. Fantasy got the best of him. (One of the characteristics of fantasy is the blurring of narrative performance and subject matter.) In the tale Tuhami acts the part of the Western hero by generously stepping aside, by bringing the lovers together, by offering advice. He plays the traditional role of the father in a marriage transaction. He even plays the fool—to be coy. The story fails. I asked him—unaware, at the time, of the meaning of my question—whether he had ever taken up the Spanish girl's invitation. "No," he answered. "How could I? Jean-Pierre was always in front of the house." He tried to laugh.

·   ·   ·

Several months after telling me the story of his love affair with the Berber woman, Tuhami told me that he had been to Casablanca only once; it was with his grandfather after his mother's death. He did not even remember the story of the Berber woman. Now the first woman he had ever slept with was one he met at a saint's tomb, at Moulay Bushta's sanctuary near Fez.

·   ·   ·

— I was sick in 1952. I did not work for a whole year. I spent the year in the hospital of Sidi Sa'id.* I then went to Moulay Bushta's to see the saint, and I spent three months and ten days there. I worked for a *sherif* there . . . I carried wood and grain. I helped cook. I stayed there until I learned that my sister was going to marry.† Then I left. The *sherif* did not want me to leave. Sometimes I still think about going back there. I got sick again. I could not even go to my sister's wedding.
— Did you stay at Moulay Bushta's?
— No. I had already started to work for the Muslim. Then I

*See footnote on page 57.
†This is the only mention Tuhami ever made of his sister's marriage.

got sick and went to Sidi 'Ali's. I spent a month there—and slept in the sanctuary.

— How did you eat?

— Eating was not important.

— Why did you leave?

— They let me leave. I went back to the Moroccan's factory in Meknes. I was never sick again.

The identity of the "they" who let Tuhami leave is not at all clear. Saint? *Jinn*? Tuhami was of course sick again: "Sometimes I still think about going back there."

— Do you visit Sidi 'Ali's sanctuary now?

— From time to time. I also go to Moulay Idriss's sanctuary and to Fez—to Moulay Idriss's there, to Sidi 'Ali Bughaleb's, to Sidi Ahmed Tijani's, to Sidi Hamamush's. I visit them every year.

— When did you begin to visit them?

— When I was first sick. In the hospital I did not know the saints. I only knew them later on, when the king returned from exile.

Here Tuhami implies that he was sick twice, first when he was in the hospital and later when he visited the saints. He claims to have left the hospital in 1952 or 1953. He claims not to have known the saints until the king's return from exile in 1955. The two illnesses are confused.

— How did you get sick?

— I was working one night in the factory, pushing a dolly. Suddenly someone called me. I turned around, and someone threw a rock and hit me between the shoulders. My knees and head hurt afterward. I went to Shaykh el-Kamal, but it did not help. Then I went to the hospital. Even now my knees hurt me.

(*In this version, Tuhami mentions neither his grandfather nor Mme Jolan. He uses a masculine form for "someone."*)

— Who threw the rock?

— The man was invisible. I could not see his face when he threw it. . . . When I was sick, I dreamed of a woman. She was a little black. She was dressed in blue, white, red, and yellow. After I had the dream of a woman, I went to see Moulay Ahmed, a very old man. He was 120 years old—a descendant of Moulay

'Ali Sherif [the father of the founder of the present 'Alawite dynasty]. Moulay Ahmed told me what the dream meant and told me to visit Sidi Buker bel 'Arabi, Sidi 'Ayed Susi, Sidi 'Amar . . . .

(*Tuhami then listed twenty saints. He seemed to have lost track of his story.*)

— What was the dream?

— The woman told me to dress like her. She told me to do what she does and to do everything she says. I did not know who the woman was until I went to Sidi 'Ali.

(*Tuhami's implication is that the woman was 'A'isha Qandisha. Her grotto is under a giant fig tree near Sidi 'Ali's tomb.*)

— Where did you have the dream?

— At home.

— Did you wake up?

— No. In the morning I went to the place where the dream took place. If I dream about a river or a saint, I always go there. I dreamed I was at Sidi 'Ali's, and so I went there. I went to Lalla 'A'isha's grotto there. I took candles and slept there. I dreamed of Lalla 'A'isha. She told me that . . . .

Tuhami stopped. He was very nervous. Mentioning Lalla 'A'isha is always dangerous. One can never be sure when the she-demon will attack. Tuhami rarely called her, or any of the other demons, by name, and, when he did, I had the feeling that it was only to make the subject of his recitation clearer to me, a foreigner. I do not think he would have used her name so cavalierly to a fellow Moroccan. His need to go to "a river or a saint" about whom he had dreamed is not unusual. The dream is interpreted as a message—a command, really—from the *jinn* or saint (Crapanzano 1975). It must be followed. If it is not, the dreamer will suffer dire consequences.

— The day I dreamed of the woman in black, I went to Moulay Ahmed. He wrote out an amulet for me to put around my neck. He was sick for six months after that. I wanted to hang it around my neck, but Lalla 'A'isha told me not to wear it. . . .

Tuhami suggests here that Lalla 'A'isha made Moulay Ahmed sick. Although the she-demon is always hostile to the *fuqaha*, the magician-teachers who prepare amulets, phylacteries, and other apotropaic devices against the *jnun*, she does not discourage her husbands, followers, or victims from visiting saints' tombs and sanctuaries. Her cult is linked to the cult of saints. The Hamadsha saints are thought to have some control over her. Tuhami has called Sidi Ahmed her commander.

— I visited all the saints and felt better afterward. I spent about three months at this before I went to the hospital of Sidi Sa'id. I spent all this time visiting saints, but I got even worse. (*Tuhami was very confused.*) Then I went to the hospital, but I didn't want to stay. I finally escaped after a year.
— Why did you go to the hospital?
— I fainted in the house and was taken to the hospital. Otherwise I would never have gone.
— Who took you?
— The Muslim.
— Had you ever fainted before?
— No. They never told me anything in the hospital.
— What was wrong?
— My knees hurt. I could not walk. It was very painful. Every night I was there, I dreamed of Lalla 'A'isha. She told me to leave. I dreamed I was fighting with people, and she was always on my side. So I always won my battles.
— What else did she tell you?
— A lot. But I can't say.
— Whom were you fighitng?
— The *jnun.* (*Tuhami lowered his voice. It is very dangerous to mention the* jnun *by name rather than through paraphrasis.*)
— What were they like?
— There were some with horns and others without horns. There were some with slippers and others without slippers. There were some with hair and others without hair. All of the *jnun* were men. The women were on my side.

Tuhami paused. He was dazed. His relations with men and women had been graphically expressed. Men were the enemy. Women were his protection—but not without cost. He was also 'A'isha Qandisha's victim. She was associated, indirectly here, with his illness. It was a man who threw the stone, but Tuhami's associations led directly to the she-demon.*

---

*The saints—males—are also a source of protection. In many legends, however, most notably those of the Hamadsha saints (Crapanzano 1973), they are associated with female attributes.

— What was it like in the hospital?

— They gave me shots and pills. Sometimes the doctors would talk to me for a few minutes. They gave me a room all to myself.

— Was it locked?

— No.

— How did you leave the hospital?

— In the night. I didn't say anything. My nurse didn't even know. My knees didn't hurt me. I went to Shaykh el-Kamal's and spent the night there. Lalla 'A'isha came to me that night and told me not to go back to the hospital. I went back to my room at the Muslim's the next day. I rested for a week and went back to work.

Tuhami's return from the hospital bears little resemblance to the return mentioned in his previous recitation. There he was greeted with a celebration; here, with work. In both instances, however, he is in the company of women: Mme Jolan and her sister and daughters, 'A'isha Qandisha and her many manifestations. Notice how he articulates his desire not to return to the hospital in terms of the she-demon's command.

— Did anyone from the hospital come looking for you?

— No. I felt much better. About a week later I was in my room and dreamed that a man came to me and told me to visit Moulay Bushta. I dreamed I was at Moulay Bushta's side.

— Who was the man?

— The man was Lhadi. He was the *muqaddim* [the caretaker] at Moulay Bushta's sanctuary.

— Had you ever seen him before?

— No. I left early the next day for Moulay Bushta's. It took two days. When I got there, I walked around the saint's tomb and spent three days there. And then I went to Moulay 'Ali Zahara's.

— Did you have any dreams at Moulay Bushta's sanctuary?

It is very common for a pilgrim to go to a saint's tomb in order to have a dream, which is interpreted as a visitation from the saint (Crapanzano 1975). What the saint reveals in the dream is taken for the truth. What the saint orders must be followed. Often, at certain sanctuaries, pilgrims will often remain for days, months, and even years, waiting for such a dream.

— I dreamed I was in Meknes—that I would return to Meknes. I spent three months and ten days at Moulay 'Ali Zahara's. I arrived, walked around the saint's tomb, and later I cooked for the people there and carried firewood.

— Who sent you there?

— Moulay Bushta. A black man came and told me to go to Moulay 'Ali Zahara's. It was a Friday night. He worked at Moulay Bushta's. His name was Ahmed ben 'Abdullah. He receives gifts for the saint. When I was at Moulay 'Ali's, I wanted to go back to Meknes, but every morning my knees hurt. I could not walk.

— Did you have any dreams at Moulay 'Ali's?

— No.

— How did you leave?

— I dreamed (!) I had to go to Moulay Bushta's to lodge a complaint against Moulay 'Ali because he would not let me leave. The next morning, after the dream, I lit a fire, warmed some water for my ablutions, and prepared coffee. I saw a man called Qaddur in front of me. He was the *muqaddim* at Moulay 'Ali's; he died later in Mekka. He told me that Moulay 'Ali had said good-bye to me. After breakfast I left for Fez. I spent a month there, at Sidi 'Ali Bughaleb's and Sidi Ahmed Tijani's.

— Did you have dreams there?

— No.

— How did you leave?

— I was asleep in front of Sidi 'Ali Bughaleb's tomb. A man walked out of the sancturary and told me to leave and go on with my work. I had never seen him before. (*Tuhami then stretched—to close the conversation.*)

•   •   •

Tuhami is entrapped. He is a victim of a male *jinn* whom he associates immediately, through the memory of a dream, with 'A'isha Qandisha, a *jinniyya*, possessing distinctly male attributes. She offers him protection from the male *jnun*. He is able to leave the hospital. He expresses, through her, his presumed desire not to return to the hospital; this may also be a way of defending himself against a desire to return to the hospital. His removal from the "real" world was not without its compensations. The fact remains, however, that 'A'isha Qandisha, a female, mediates his desire to live and work in the male world. Her mediation is less than satisfactory. Tuhami is her victim. He must obey her. He must remain passive, like a woman, before her. He dreams, after only a week, of a man who instructs him to visit a male saint. He has no choice but to follow the man's—the saint's—command. Otherwise, according to prevalent belief, he will suffer harm. He does not have to give his reason for visiting the saint's sanctuary, for his flight from the male *jnun*—or from 'A'isha Qandisha—to the sanctuary, which is symbolically equivalent to the hospital. It, too, is separate and offers the possibility of cure.

Tuhami's attitude toward the saints is again one of passivity. He must obey their commands, whether those commands are manifested directly (through a dream) or indirectly, through one of the saint's spokesmen, a *muqaddim,* or a caretaker. Tuhami moves from sanctuary to sanctuary. He cries for release. He dreams of lodging a complaint against the saint, Moulay 'Ali Zahara, to another saint, Moulay Bushta. Finally he is released. He returns to Meknes. Curiously, he does not mention the dream that has released him from saintly bondage until I ask him specifically about it. He tells the dream indifferently, stereotypically: "a man walked out of the sanctuary and told me to leave and go on with my work." His recitation ran out—for the moment. His pilgrimages, and his recitations of his pilgrimages, were to continue.

Part Two

Tuhami is caught between the male saint and the female *jinniyya*, and, despite his intense "involvement" with both figures, he receives neither support nor release from them. As I have suggested elsewhere (1973), the saint and the *jinniyya* are symbolic-interpretive elements through which, *under certain circumstances,* the Moroccans of Tuhami's background articulate their experience of reality. They are not simple figures of allegory but complex symbols with rich associative auras. They have both sociocultural and personal-psychological referents. Insofar as these symbolic-interpretive elements are part of a system, they are subject to the logical constraints and evaluations of that system, and they serve to structure and evaluate (the articulated) experience. As male and female, they resonate not only with traditional sociocultural stereotypes of man and woman in Morocco but with the individual's experience of men and women generally and, specifically (if we accept a psychoanalytic bias), of father and mother. In a world that is dramatically cleft into male and female, they are particularly eloquent symbols of opposition and conflict. They afford, too, at the symbolic level, the resolution of opposition and conflict (Crapanzano 1977c).

To look at the saint and *jinniyya* as simply symbols, of whatever status, is, however, to lose sight of their most important feature for the Moroccan: their facticity, their givenness in and for themselves. Both saint and *jinniyya* manifest themselves in dreams, visions, and other states of consciousness. The saint is a "historical" personage who is believed to be alive within his sanctuary and whose existence is confirmed through action—his miraculous interventions in ordinary life. The *jinniyya*'s existence is also confirmed through action.

As givens that can intervene in ordinary human life, the saint and the *jinniyya* must be taken into account and relations with them ordered. Much of Tuhami's life is in fact an attempt to modify his relations with various saints and with 'A'isha Qandisha and her many refractions. He hopes, through establishing a bond with a saint, to achieve the power to overcome 'A'isha Qandisha or at least to diminish her enslaving hold over him. Curiously, he rejects the one mechanism that is considered most efficacious in his milieu: the trance-dance of the Hamadsha.

The Hamadsha cure involves a symbolic structuring—or restructuring—of those feelings and sentiments that are identified in Morocco, through male saints and female demons, with maleness and femaleness. Feelings of inadequacy, impotence, passivity—of not being able to live up to the highest standards of male behavior—are identified with being like a woman. The male saint provides the female demon's victim with the necessary power, strength, and virility to overcome her, first by giving her symbolic expression (in the victim's state of possession) and then by agreeing to live up to her commands. So long as the commands, often symbolic of living up to the expected standards of male behavior, are followed, the male victim of a female *jinn* will in fact live up to those standards. The conflict between adequacy and inadequacy, potency and impotence, superiority and inferiority, aggressiveness and passivity, maleness and femaleness, animus and anima—it matters little what idiom we use here—is expressed and resolved on a stage external to the individual. This symbolic expression and resolution of conflict has the singular advantage of shifting responsibility from self to saint and demon, who resonate with feelings and sentiments grounded within the personal history of the individual. The saints and demons remove the burden of failure, of guilt even. It is *they* who command.

The relations that obtain between saint, *jinniyya*, and human beings are articulated in the same manner as those that obtain between human beings, and the steps taken to alter these relations are also similar in both situations. In making this observation I do not wish to reduce, in Durkheimian fashion, the religious to the social. However satisfying such a maneuver may be to the Westerner—it spares him, after all, the confrontation with the religious—it would hardly be satisfactory to the Moroccan, who, if he were to bother, would probably argue the very

opposite, namely, that social relations are modeled on the relations that obtain between saints, demons, and human beings.
The important point here is not the priority of explanation—
both sides have vested interests—but the fact that the relations
are articulated in the same way and serve, I believe, in a complex
dialectical manner to underscore and reinforce each other both
cognitively and affectively.

Moroccan social organization, Rosen has written, seems "to
center around the relations between pairs of individuals, each of
whom is perceived as a concatenation of particular social ties and
cultural traits which are differently weighted and apportioned
from one individual to another" (Rosen 1972, p. 443). The individual, or the person, rather than the corporate group is at the
center of such organization. To be sure, there are social
groups—kin groups, religious confraternities, guilds, and the
like; but these groups do not appear to be as carefully defined,
as imposing, as they are both in the West and, further south, in
Africa. They are, in Rosen's words, "minimally corporate."
Membership, itself ill-defined, does not rigidly prescribe modes
of behavior, but it does limit, up to a certain point, the range of
flexibility an individual has in managing his relations with
others. It also provides him, *on occasion,* with a series of rhetorical, political, and economic strategies for accomplishing certain
of his ends.

> ...each individual, using both the minimal rights and duties
> associated with his inherent positions and a wide range of
> personal, contractual, and often *ad hoc* ties to others, forges a
> network of affiliations and has attributed to him by others a
> series of valued personal characteristics which will be as indi-
> vidually distinctive in their particular patterning for any one
> person as they will be socially typical in the ways in which they
> will have been formed and attributed. Throughout his life
> each man, free from an elaborate set of binding obligations to
> the members of the groups into which he is born, will derive
> his identity from that highly personalized network of associa-
> tions which he himself will have constructed. [Ibid., p. 437]

The Moroccan, Rosen observes (p. 441), following Schutz (1962,
1967), tends to regard his contemporaries as bound together in a
"chain of consociation." Two individuals, in other words, who
have never come into direct face-to-face contact, who are not,

strictly-speaking, consociates, "are regarded as linked together through a specifiable series of intermediate face-to-face contacts."

This mode of social organization gives the individual more flexibility, more freedom even, in the management of his social relations than he might have in more corporate organizations. It renders his social life more personable—cloying, even, to the Westerner—and subject to greater scheming, intriguing, and manipulation. Each and every individual one encounters is of potential benefit, either directly or as an intermediary (*wasita*), and must be bound into a relationship through an act—a gift, a favor, a gesture of hospitality, a greeting even, or the expression of concern—that demands reciprocation.

The giving of gifts, Mauss (1967) noted, bears with it the obligation to reciprocate. Such reciprocation need be neither immediate nor in kind. However, there is always the expectation of a return, accompanied by a certain security that derives from such expectations. There is always the possibility, too, that the obligation (*haqq*) will not be met. Social pressure, as well as internalized standards of appropriate behavior, insofar as they exist, mitigates this danger. As elsewhere in the Mediterranean, proper social comportment is symbolized by an expression—in Moroccan Arabic, *hshumiyya*—that connotes shame. *Hshumiyya* is best translated as "propriety," but it includes within its range of meanings "deference," "respect," "circumspection," and "embarrassment" (Eikelman 1976). "The locus of propriety," Eikelman writes, "is not so much the moral consciousness of a person as his public comportment with respect to those with whom he has regular face-to-face relations." Indeed, as I have remarked with respect to the Hamadsha (Crapanzano 1972, 1973), psychological guilt consequent upon the internalization of standards of moral behavior is not particularly in evidence. Given this "public" locus of propriety, public or semipublic exposure helps to insure reciprocation. A serious breach of obligation can lead to the placing of an *'ar*, a compulsion, or, as Westermarck (1926, vo.. 1) would have it, a "conditional curse," on the person who has failed to live up to his obligations. In extremely serious cases an *'ar* may involve sacrificing a sheep before the door of the person being compelled or placing a daughter or infant in his protection. More often it involves a public gift of a large amount of sugar. An *'ar* must always be performed in public (see Eikelman 1976, pp. 149–53). The sacrifice of a chicken, goat, or sheep, or even the gift of sugar or candles to a saint, are referred to as an *'ar*. They are thought to impose an obligation (*haqq*, which may also mean "truth") on the saint to respond favorably to the supplicant's request. Like tying a cloth to a tree sacred to the saint (or, for that matter, to 'A'isha Qandisha), an act also referred to as an *'ar*, they bind the supplicant to further sacrifice or gifts if his request is met. Sacrifice is the ultimate compulsion in Moroccan social organization and its symbolic keystone.

There is a precariousness, a fundamental insecurity, in such a flexible, particularistic mode of life.* There is the constant threat that the bonds of reciprocation will dissolve. Persons who exchange with each other are called *shab*, "companions," "associates," "friends"; but as Eikelman notes (1976, p. 144), *shab* carries no necessary connotation of deep affective relations. Indeed, Eikelman, not without some justice, goes so far as to suggest that in Moroccan society affective relations are "decidedly subordinate to relations of obligation." Relations are continually negotiated and renegotiated (Rabinow 1975). There is, accordingly, an illusive, literally intangible, quality to Moroccan life; no act, however gratuitous, is without rhetorical significance. Interpreting a sequence of behavior is like unraveling a complex arabesque. Stories, and not only Tuhami's recitations, ramify endlessly, seem never to come to the climax, the *dénouement*, that is so critical to Western appreciation.

In his analysis of Moroccan social relations, Rosen (1972) stresses the competitive element, which he equates with a struggle for dominance and dependence. Eikelman (1976, p. 143) argues that dominance is coveted because it allows a man to be autonomous, to assert his claim as a full social person, and to maintain his social honor. The dominant partner in the relationship is said to have the word (*kelma*). There is no doubt that

---

*This precariousness may well bring about a turning to Islam, as it did for Hadj Brahim in Waterbury's study of the Susi merchant: "Hadj Brahim assumes the fragility of human relations and inconsistency of human roles and seeks the predictability and consistency that would otherwise be lacking in his life in Islam" (Waterbury 1972, p. 155). The insecurity of which I am speaking results from social relations both within and outside the extended family. I am not arguing, as Gulick (1973) does, that ambivalence, hostility, jealousy, and distrust within the family are necessarily responsible for an "ethos of insecurity."

there is a strong competitive element in all social relations, involving considerable jockeying for power and prestige, at least among those who can aspire to power and prestige. However, those who have the word, with all of its autonomy, assertions of personhood, and honor, also stand in very real danger of being isolated. The dominant, as Hegel (1966 ed.) noted in his analysis of the master-slave relationship, is himself dependent upon the subordinate.* The reasonable individual in Morocco seeks flexible relations of both dominance and dependence. Ultimately it is only the king (and traditionally, at the local level, the *pasha* and the *qa'id*) who has the final word, and this accounts for the symbolic value of his position. (It may also account for a certain arbitrariness associated with his position.) Rosen and Eikelman notwithstanding, there is, then, in Moroccan social life a strong impulsion not only to seek the word but to bind oneself to those who have it. The seeking of relations of dependence has, of course, both social and psychological consequences (Mannoni 1956). It is particularly important among the urban poor, who seldom have access to the word and thus seek what security they can in relations of dependence with those, including saints and demons, who do have access to it. This impulsion toward dependence receives more general expression, I suggest, in an egalitarianism, often confusing to the Westerner, that exists in Morocco amidst great and manifest discrepancies of wealth and power, prestige and rank.

The great stress placed on establishing and maintaining particular social relations permits a relativist attitude toward questions of truth.† The Moroccan will often appear to the outsider to contradict—even to lie—as he describes a sequence of events or his goals to different interlocutors or even to the same interlocutor on different occasions. He does not seem particularly concerned about contradictions of this kind, and he does not dwell upon them with guilt or remorse. Truth is seen, rather, in a relationally determined contextual framework. Up to a certain point, a greater value is placed on the relationship that is sought

---

*Mannoni (1956) also notes that the dependent take possession, at least psychologically, of those upon whom they are dependent.

†A similar argument can be advanced for a relativist approach to matters of right and wrong. This position is expressed in the gradations of right and wrong conduct recognized by Islamic law (Levy 1962).

than on the circumstances that surround it or even its ostensible goal. (It is with regard to the latter that the goal-oriented instrumentality inherent in the competitive model of Moroccan social relations fails; for, *always within certain limits,* the maintenance of the relationship is given greater value than the immediate goal sought through the relationship.) Circumstances and goals become rhetorical devices for establishing and maintaining the relationship and the security that may derive from them. There are of course "real" and conventional limits to such rhetorical strategies. The Moroccans, as many observers have remarked, are pragmatists who are well aware of the risks in their rhetorical play with truth.

Tuhami's evocative play with his own personal history, with his life, even, may be seen as an extreme example of this attitude toward truth. His several confusing versions of what followed the death of his father, for example, are attempts, I believe, to establish, evocatively, through me, his interlocutor, his own identity, even his worth. Tuhami is in many respects the contemporary Moroccan *in extremis.* He is both unique and a stereotype. His is a victim of allegorical proportions, of a shattered mode of social life that was tradtionally not without its casualties. The particularistic, highly flexible mode of traditional social organization, which, to be sure, had its virtues, offered little security, especially to the great mass of powerless and impoverished, who constituted the majority of the people of the *makhzan,* and at times it offered not even the requisite stability to develop a strong sense of personal identity and self-worth. Even before the arrival of the French and the Spanish, Moroccan society rested on harsh and arbitrary exploitation.

There were, of course, great and noble virtues, most notably the Islamic injunction to charity, that helped to mitigate the severity of life. (I do not in any way want to underplay the importance of Islamic values in traditional Morocco.) There were also traditional modes of coping with personal as well as social crises. The saints and the *jnun* mirrored, not without realistic ambiguity, the stable and constant, the unstable and inconstant, aspects of social relations. The saint could be bound, when necesary through an *'ar,* to support, protect, and bless the supplicant—to bestow his *baraka.* The *jnun,* at least the named *jnun,* could be converted through the rituals of the religious confraternities—the Hamadsha, the Jilala, and the 'Isawa—and by other means as well, from arbitrary, whimsical, malevolent demons to supportive, benevolent protectors (Crapanzano 1973). The other *jnun*—the majority, the unnamed—could be exorcised, at least for a while. Saints and even converted *jnun* could provide more or less constant orientation points within the flux of everyday life; they could embody, too, the constant Other in the dialectics of identity formation (Crapanzano 1977a). 'A'isha Qandisha, for example, puts a full stop to the essentially dialectical movement of identity formation in Tuhami and other Moroccans whom she holds in her grasp. She demands from them, inevitably, stasis, impotence, illness, and even death as the price for an identity that to the Westerner, at least, seems illusory. Above all, saints and *jnun* enabled the articulation of reality and the expression of fantasy in a shared symbolic vocabulary that allowed the individual to transcend his embeddedness in immediate reality—to generalize his circumstances—and to take what solace he could from such transcendence (Munn 1973).

With the arrival of the Spanish and the French and the subsequent colonialization of Morocco, traditional patterns of behavior and the confidence the Moroccan had in his symbolically constituted world were undermined, not, in most instances, suddenly and dramatically, but gradually and irregularly, subtly. (Morocco, in its long history, has often been subject to outside influence and incursion.) The meaning and efficacy of symbols were altered if not lost altogether (Geertz 1968; Rabinow 1975). Ritual symbols—symbols more generally—Nancy Munn has written, "are testaments to the joining of individuals in objective social relationships that have personal subjective relevance and internalized normative value" (Munn 1973, p. 582). They fail when they no longer imply this sort of relationship. The symbols may still serve to articulate the universe but will lack the immediacy they once may have had. Fragmented, they present a less coherent, a less cohesive, even a contradictory picture of the world. (One must always temper such assertions, for our own Edenic myth may interfere with our perceptions and influence our judgments.) They become, at least secondarily, symbols of separation and alienation.

Tuhami is, as I have said, a victim of this shattered mode of social life. He is both more traditional and less traditional than

Tuhami's sickness
is sickness of man caught in change ore from colonial to post-colonial.

many Moroccans of his background. He insists upon articulating his world in traditional symbols, but he is unable to receive succor from such symbolic understanding. He is haunted by demons—enslaved by them—but is incapable of receiving ritual release from them. Why ? The question must be asked, and it cannot be answered without imposing a determinism on Tuhami that would deprive him of what freedom he has. He is, despite everything, capable of manipulating the symbol system, however fragmented and alienating it may be, to his advantage. Perhaps he does not want the cure. Perhaps, like the hero (or rather antihero) in Dostoevski's *Notes from the Underground*, he derives benefit, a secondary gain, from being a victim. This possibility must be entertained.

And yet—and perhaps this is my Western presumption—I see Tuhami as more passive before the saints and *jnun* than the Western neurotic is before his symbolic benefactors and persecutors. I believe him to be out of his depth. His saints and his demons are, in their obstinate facticity, resistant to the new referents that colonialism and modernization have brought to him and to other Moroccans. They may become static emblems of new and complex figures and events in Tuhami's life—of Mme Jolan, for example, and her ambivalent relations with him—but they cannot do justice to the novelty and complexity of these figures and events. They can only freeze in a simplified order what is neither simple nor static. Ritual symbols, Nancy Munn (1973) suggests, "release the relevant shared meanings embedded in the cultural code into the level of ongoing social process"; they provide "external templates for inner experience" that "work back" on that experience. Ritual operations—and these would include the cures that Tuhami refuses—are aimed at adjusting internal orientations to objective social processes and immediate reality. They adjust the individual's perception of the possibilities inherent in his situation and his orientation toward that situation. Where, however, as in Tuhami's case, there is no longer any relevance in the cultural code to the "ongoing social process," there can be no adjustment. The gap is too great. The individual is destined either to lead his life in terms of the frozen symbols of the now irrelevant cultural code—or idiom, as I prefer to call it—or to be cast adrift in the flux of meaningless social activity.

Tuhami opted, I believe, for the frozen symbols of an irrelevant idiom. His recitations reaffirm the collectively sanctioned but, for him at least, defunct structure that he has adopted for himself; they enable him—and here perhaps his freedom enters—to be exceptional within the collectivity. They make it possible for him to recite what could otherwise not have been cited. Paradoxically, the recitations served contradictory functions (mediated over time by me). On the one hand, they confirmed Tuhami's stance of being as if dead; they were simply repetitions. (Repetition is an attempt to abolish time. . . .) Like Sartre's (1964) Genet, Tuhami deigned "to take notice of the circumstances of his life only insofar as they seem to repeat the original drama of his loss of Paradise." They were, in their repetition, also symbols of the defunct idiom Tuhami employed. On the other hand, Tuhami's recitations were an attempt to resurrect the life that had died with his flight from the Jolan family, with the death of his parents, with the move to Meknes (events symbolically merged for Tuhami). They were, as such, idiosyncratic rituals, magical displays, gentle subterfuges, violent seductions. In a way they were confidence games in which Tuhami—momentarily and through his interlocutor—became his own fall guy. They were symbolic, too, of his attempt to vitalize his idiom. Here the parallel with the *baraka*-giving pilgrimages is especially striking.*

Tuhami's recitations are, I believe, compulsive analogues of his obsessive pilgrimages. Both the recitations and the pilgrimages serve in their distinct ways to remove Tuhami from the constraints of everyday life and to plunge him into a liminal world that affords him a certain privilege. Victor Turner (1974) has stressed the difference between ordinary social life, subject to the constraints of status and role, and "the total process of pilgrimage." The pilgrimage permits a routinized but unstructured and undifferentiated communion, a "normative communitas," as Turner puts it somewhat awkwardly, of equal

---

*It is possible to argue here that the two paradoxical functions of Tuhami's recitations—the confirmation of being dead and the attempt at resurrection— exploit the two aspects of a recitation. A recitation is both a text and a performance. The one, which corresponds in Saussurean linguistics to *langue*, is timeless and static, dead; the other, which corresponds to *parole*, is written within time and dynamic, alive.

individuals. Social structure is not eliminated but radically simplified; genetic rather than particularistic relationships are
stressed. The pilgrimage center represents "a threshold, a place
and moment 'in and out of time.'" (The pilgrim "is no longer
involved in that combination of historical and social structural
time which constitutes the social process in his rural or urban
community" [p. 207]). The pilgrim hopes to have "direct experience of the sacred, invisible, or supernatural order, either in the
material aspect of miraculous healing or in the immaterial aspect
of inward transformation of spirit or personality" (p. 197). Or, I
would add, *both* healing and spiritual transformation; the two
are not so easily differentiated. The pilgrim's route, as he pro-
gresses, becomes increasingly sacralized "til almost every land-
mark and ultimately every step is a condensed multivocal symbol
capable of arousing much affect and desire" (p. 198). "No longer
is the pilgrim's sense of the sacred private; it is a matter of
objectified, collective representations which become virtually his
whole environment and give him powerful motives for cre-
dence" (p. 198).

Through the pilgrimage, which Turner likens to a *rite de passage*, "solitude and society cease to be antithetical" (p. 203); vol-
untariness and obligation are united in a sort of Kantian com-
promise (p. 175); the inner meaning of the pilgrim's culture is
more intensely realized (p. 208); the journey, itself of mythic
proportions, becomes a paradigm for ethical, political, and other
kinds of behavior (p. 198). The pilgrim comes to participate in a
sacred existence and becomes even "a total symbol, indeed a
symbol of totality" (p. 208).

Although Turner's account appears to me to be rather too
Christian, certainly too idealized (at least with respect to the
ordinary Moroccan *zyara*, or visit to a saint's sanctuary), it does
call attention to certain faundamental features of the pilgrimage
that permit Tuhami the same privilege he finds in his recitations.
Both the pilgrimage and the recitation afford him a certain
freedom from the constraints of everyday life. Both remove him
from the "combination" of historical and social-structural time.
In the recitations he enters narrative time but remains, too, in
the time of performance. In the pilgrimage he is "in and out of
time"; or, rather, he is in that special time of pilgrimage that is
both contemporary and constructed—at least ideally—on a transcendent and only partially articulated plot. He is permitted, in

both, free play between the resistance of reality and the conventions of plot. He is in different ways a hero. Aside from whatever identifications he may make with the legendary personages of the pilgrimage,* Tuhami was, with his immense repertoire of magic, lore, and tale, always a center of attention at the pilgrimage centers he visited. They were the *loci optimi* for his recitations! I remember accompanying him on several visits to saints' tombs in and near Meknes. He was immediately recognized and warmly greeted by the caretakers and regular visitors, both of whom appeared exceptionally interested in what he had to say.)

In both pilgrimage and recitation Tuhami undergoes a transformation—in fact, a complexly interrelated double transformation. On the one hand, by means of the performance, he is transformed from an ordinary social personage into either a pilgrim or a bard; on the other hand, within the performance, as an actor within a "literary" or transcendent plot, he undergoes, or better still, hopes to undergo, a transformation that will extend beyond his special performance into ordinary life. In the case of the pilgrimage, his hope is sanctioned by collective belief; in the case of the recitation, his hope has no such sanction and is in fact illusory. Illusions and failure are masked by his confusing transformation by performance with transformation in performance. In both instances, aside from whatever benefits accrue to him from the performances themselves, Tuhami is able to objectify certain feeling states in terms that transcend him. He is able, in other words, to generalize his situation and to reap, I suppose, some benefit from such objectification and generalization. Neither his recitations nor his pilgrimages afford him ultimately the symbolic renewal that is, I believe, requisite for true spiritual and curative transformation. He becomes, in both, a symbol, but hardly a vitalizing symbol, of totality. Rather, he becomes a contextually determined and delimited symbol, frozen, so to speak, within a text that affords only illusory transformation and renewal through repetition. He experiences no real passage. He is caught like the madman on the medieval ship

---

*Neither Tuhami nor any other Moroccan I ever talked to intimated that such identifications occur in the *zyara*.

of fools, the *stultifera navis,* the *Narrenschiff,* in passage. His position is, as I have written, not without a certain privilege.

Tuhami returns again and again to illness in his recitations. Illness is not simply an event in the course of his life. Illnesses are condensed into one ultimate illness, existing, insofar as possible, not in the real but in mythic time, *in illo tempore,* as Eliade (1954) puts it. It is a citation whose real-life referent has ceased to be of significance. (Sartre [1964] notes for Genet that the event that determined *his* fate had long ceased to be a memory and had entered the category of myths.) Illness for Tuhami is a symbolic mediator: being-alive-yet-dead, being-dead-yet-alive. It cannot be situated too precisely because then it would carry the possibility of history, of the real, of idiosyncratic desire as opposed to the constricted desire that is manifestly expressed in his recitations. Illness symbolizes for Tuhami a stance toward life that had become petrified. It also marks a change that precludes future change: a switch, outside time, from movement to stasis, from the "real" to the mythic, the symbolic, the *recited,* and thus defunct code—from being alive to being dead. It provides, too, the possibility for the privilege of liminality; of passage, by performance and not in performance; of repetition within time that at the same time abolishes time; of choice without choice.

Part Three

Tuhami, like most Moroccans of his milieu, attended both the public and private ceremonies of the Hamadsha and other popular brotherhoods. I never saw him at a private ceremony, but more than once I did see him alone on a Friday afternoon in the square, in front of the sanctuary of the Perfect Shaykh, Sidi Mohammed ben 'Isa, the founder of the 'Isawa brotherhood. The square was then a sort of miniature Jma' el Fna, the famous square of Marrakech. There Tuhami could watch the Hamadsha perform their public dances—dances that were therapeutically less efficacious than the private ceremonies but were theatrically more spectacular and certainly bloodier. There, too, he could watch the white-robed 'Isawa dance with an almost hypnotic grace to the whining music of their oboes. (The 'Isawa, in this particular ceremony, always reminded me of the whirling dervishes of the eastern Mediterranean.) And he could watch the Miliana, who danced with burning torches and occasionally lapped up the flames with their tongues, or the Hnayshiyya, a branch of the 'Isawa who played with highly venomous snakes. (The Perfect Shaykh is said to have concluded a pact with snakes and vipers.) Or he could listen to a professional storyteller, a bard, tell of the days of the Prophet, of the great religious wars, of the glory of the Islamic past and the splendour of the palaces of kings and sultans. He could receive the blessing of a wandering *sherif*, a holy man who claimed descent from the Prophet, give a few francs to a poor beggar (and thus gain recognition from the angel who sat on his right shoulder and counted his good deeds), watch with skeptical amazement the old man who puffed out his lungs through a hole in his chest or one of the several cardsharps who always managed to dupe some ingenuous stranger from the country. He liked to listen to the prophecies of the holy fools, the *mejdubin*, the Moroccan's equivalent of the *saloi* of Old Russia (Fedotov 1966), and to those put forth by members of the mendicant brotherhoods. I particularly remember him standing in front of a frail old man, who, having seated himself, fakir-like, on a tiny scrap of oilcloth, proceeded to weep; occasionally the old man would gesture wildly with his staff.

•   •   •

Once I asked Tuhami if he were ever carried away by the trance-dances of the Hamadsha.

— When I see the Hamadsha dance, my heart begins to throb; but I have never danced.

— Why?

— I don't want to. (*Tuhami's voice was cold and emphatic.*) You cannot say I am really carried away. The dances of the Jilala and the Gnawa have no effect upon me. My body does not tremble when I hear the 'Isawa beat their chests.

[During certain 'Isawa dances, men—they are called lions— beat their chests like drums to the rhythm of the music. Their chests are always raw by the end of the dance.]

I sweat a lot then, but I'm not carried away. If someone laughs at the dancers, then I fall into a rage and want to kill him.

— When did this happen?

— Last year.

— What happened?

— Some men were laughing at the 'Isawa and at the enrapt spectators. They will fall into a trap. Laughing like that! (*Tuhami was very upset.*) Such men do not think they have done anything. Then perhaps one day they'll go to a spring for a drink and they will be struck. (*Tuhami laughed.*) [The *jnun* are thought to gravitate to springs.] Or perhaps they will kick a stone or a scrap of iron as they are walking at night. They will have touched one of the invisibles and will pay for their laughter.

[Tuhami suggests that, by kicking metals, thought to be frightening to the *jnun*, the men will become particularly vulnerable to demonic attack. Stones may be the haunt of the *jnun*.]

— What happened when you fell into a rage?

— My heart began to throb. My head became very heavy. I didn't want anyone to talk to me.

Tuhami grew silent. He eyed me evasively. I felt myself the object of his rage—the object of the rage he felt at not being able to submit to the rituals of a brotherhood that might perhaps be of help to him.* He had not received the calling. Its idiom was corporeal. At the time, I did not ask myself why his rage was directed at me. Now I think that I may have symbolized both the man—always the unnamed man—and the European who held him back, who taught him to be mistrustful of the rituals but had not succeeded in removing the need for them. Tuhami announced that he was going to Fez. I asked why. He said angrily, "Just so."

On another occasion I asked Tuhami if he had ever invited the Hamadsha or any other brotherhood to perform. "No. How can I? I don't have a wife who can prepare a meal. I don't have a house." Not only is the meal, the *sadaqa,* that ends the ceremony important; the ceremony itself is very much a family endeavor. It requires cooperation and sacrifice from all members of the patient's family. Tuhami had none.

— What brotherhood would you invite if you had a wife and a house?

— The Ahl Twat.

— Who are they?

— The Tuhamiyya, the Wazzaniyya.

The Ahl Twat are a branch of the Tuhamiyya or Wazzaniyya brotherhood, whose members follow the path, or *tariqa,* of the Wazzani saints. Its rituals are gentler, more mystical, than those of the Hamadsha. The Ahl Twat themselves were traditionally Saharan Berbers.†

— What do they do?

— They say a *dhikr.* They pray to Allah, to Sidina 'Isa [Jesus], Sidina Musa [Moses], Sidina Mohammed, Moulay 'Abdelsherif, Moulay Idriss Zerhouni. . . . They repeat *llah, llah, llah, llah* . . . .

---

*Several psychoanalysts who have read the manuscript of *Tuhami* have independently suggested that the rage I sensed in Tuhami was probably fright.

†When I returned to Meknes in 1973, I discovered that the sons of many of the Hamadsha had begun to follow the path of the Ahl Twat. Five years earlier, the Hamadsha had made no mention of this brotherhood.

Tuhami had never mentioned the Ahl Twat or the Wazzani brotherhood before. His real name was not suggestive of the brotherhood. It was our fifth meeting. He never mentioned them again. The *dhikr* is the litany that is chanted by the adepts of a religious brotherhood. Its performance is perfunctory among the members of the popular brotherhoods, but it is of central importance in the mystical ceremonies of the elite (Sufi) brotherhoods. For the Sufis, it refers not simply to the chants that send the adepts into ecstatic trance but to teachings that prepare the way for union or communion with the Divine.

— Why would you invite the Ahl Twat rather than any other brotherhood?
— It is my spirit [*'aqel*] that decides. Their *dhikr* is good. You do not hit your head. You proceed step by step up to the Prophet. They do not say a prayer [to get money] after each step. Only at the end. Of course, a very rich man could pay them to interrupt their *dhikr* to say a prayer for him.

Tuhami is referring to the mystical stages through which an adept advances to the Divine. Like many Moroccans of his background, he does not conceive of ecstasy as a union with Allah but as communion with the Prophet or a saint. Allah is too distant, too aloof, too removed from man. To aim for unity with Him would be vain if not blasphemous. In between the dances of the popular brotherhoods, the adepts, who are often in an entranced state, say prayers (*fathas*) for those in attendance at the ceremony. In return for this blessing, they receive a few francs, which they divide among themselves after the ceremony. In theory, the money—it is called *baraka*—is to be given to the descendants of the saint whom the adepts follow.

— Do you go to their lodge?
— Yes, sometimes.
— Are you a member of the lodge?
— No.
— Why not?
— I am between many. (*Tuhami blushed.*)
— I do not understand.
— First I was on the side of Sidi 'Ali and then Sidi Ahmed and then Sidi 'Abdullah ben Brahim, then Moulay Bushta, then

Moulay 'Ali ben Zahara, Sidi Bushkri, Sidi Ms'ud.... (*Again, Tuhami is compelled to repeat the names of the saints until I interrupt him.*)

— What do you mean, "on the side of Sidi 'Ali"?

— That comes from dreams. When I see a saint in a dream, I go to him.

— Did you dream about Sidi 'Ali?

— I dreamed first of all about Sidi 'Ali. I dreamed that a woman came to me and told me to visit Sidi 'Ali.

— Who was the woman?

— Lalla 'A'isha.

Tuhami's immediate association of the Hamadsha saint with 'A'isha Qandisha was not unusual for him or for the Hamadsha themselves. (His calling her by name *was* unusual.) The association is implicit within both ritual and legend. Sidi 'Ali is said to have ordered Sidi Ahmed to fetch the she-demon from the Sudan. According to Tuhami, who embellished the story, Sidi 'Ali once sent Sidi Ahmed with a letter to the 'Alawite saint Moulay 'Ali Sherif, who lived in the Sahara.

— Sidi 'Ali did this so that Sidi Ahmed would not witness his death. Sidi Ahmed returned early. His master was facing in the direction of Mecca. [He was dying.] Sidi 'Ali then ordered him to the Sudan. There he would find a bundle of branches tied up with a rope. Sidi Ahmed closed his eyes, and when he opened them, he was in the Sudan in front of the bundle of branches. He was to pull the rope. Sidi Ahmed pulled the rope, and Lalla 'A'isha appeared and began to follow him. Sidi Ahmed told Lalla 'A'isha that he was in a hurry, that he had left his "brother" dying. Lalla 'A'isha told him to get on her back. He did and arrived immediately at Sidi 'Ali's. Just as Sidi Ahmed and Lalla 'A'isha were climbing up the steps to Sidi 'Ali's cave, Sidi 'Ali died.

[Sidi Ahmed then washed his master's body and buried him.] He was so upset because he had not heard his saint's last words that he climbed to the top of the Jebel Zerhoun [the mountain near Meknes where the Hamadsha sanctuaries are located]. He began to cry and call out the names of the saints in the area. As he called out their names, he hit at his head with an ax.

The legend is etiological. It serves as an explanation for the head-slashing practices of the Hamadsha. It also serves as a justification for the order of visiting the two Hamadsha saints in individual pilgrimages and during the great collective pilgrimage, or *musem,* that takes place each year. Sidi 'Ali, Tuhami explained, said to his followers, as he was dying, "for Sidi Ahmed, Thursdays; for Sidi 'Ali, Fridays." Pilgrims usually visit Sidi Ahmed's sanctuary first, and then Sidi 'Ali's.* Thursday and Friday are favored days for individual pilgrimages to the sanctuaries. The annual pilgrimage begins in Sidi Ahmed's village and ends in Sidi 'Ali's.

Although Moroccan saints' legends may be etiological, they do not usually provide exemplary models for behavior (Crapanzano 1973). Saints are not emulated; they are not especially worshiped for the quality of their lives. They are worshiped for the miracles they have performed. Popular hagiographies are essentially ahistorical; they are made up of a series of stereotyped miracle stories fitted into a very loose biographical frame. They are evidence of the saint's *baraka.* They justify seeking his help—ultimately, his intercession with Allah. The saints provide nodal points within a complex symbolic system that extends well beyond them into the ordinary symbols of everyday life and into the extraordinary symbols of demonic life as well. They enable the articulation—and ritual fixation—of the individual's personal experience. They do not provide him with a complete history.

Sidi Ahmed's legend resonates with Tuhami's history. His suggestion that Sidi 'Ali sent Sidi Ahmed off so that he would not witness his death is idiosyncratic. It is emphasized by his cou-

---

*In one idiosyncratic version of the legend, Tuhami relates the order of pilgrimage to marriage. "First you have to visit Sidi Ahmed's tomb," Tuhami explained to Lhacen at their first meeting. "'If you don't visit it,' Sidi 'Ali said, 'your pilgrimage is worthless.' [Sidi Ahmed was Sidi 'Ali's student.] Once Sidi Ahmed was talking to some people. They told him to tell his master to find him a wife. The next morning Sidi Ahmed was angry [*mhiyir*]. 'Why are you angry?' Sidi 'Ali asked him, several times. Finally Sidi Ahmed said, 'I want to get married.' 'Who gave you that idea?' Sidi 'Ali asked. 'These people here,' Sidi Ahmed answered; 'they have a daughter, and they want me to marry her.' Sidi 'Ali agreed. It was after his student's marriage that he said, 'For you, Thursday; for me, Friday.'" Marriage, like the correct pilgrimage sequence, is in the order of things.

pling Sidi Ahmed's trip to see Moulay 'Ali Sherif with his trip to
the Sudan. (The former is but one of many episodes that account for the saint's *baraka*. By visiting Moulay 'Ali Sherif, Sidi
Ahmed gleaned some of the older saint's *baraka*.)

Was Tuhami absent from his father's deathbed? Can much of
his experience be accounted for by what Erik Erikson (1969) has
called the "curse"—the failure to be present at the death of a
parent and to hear his or her last words? Did he relate his failure to hear his father's last words—his loss of family con-
nectedness—to the demands of a woman? In his tale of the
pasha's son, he is a harem boy at the time of his father's death.
Sidi Ahmed was also absent from his master's death on account
of a woman—'A'isha Qandisha. In his recitations, Tuhami himself always seemed to end up in the world of the women: the
pasha's son's wives and concubines, his mother, Mme Jolan. The
saint had slashed his head in mourning for his master. Tuhami responded by attempting to overcome women and their
ways through knowledge and storytelling and not through marriage. He also called out the names of the saints—through his
pilgrimages and in his recitations. This was his mourning rite.
Like Sidi Ahmed, who was sometimes said to be married to
'A'isha Qandisha, Tuhami was married to the she-demon. Unlike
the saint, however, Tuhami was not sent off by his "father" to
fetch a woman. He could have no woman. It is significant that
Tuhami ended his version of the legend with the following
words:

— Sidi Ahmed climbed down the mountain. The people tried
to comfort him. They told him he was lucky to be alive—to have
children. These children would carry on his blood and sanctity,
his *baraka*. They told him not to be angered or saddened. "You
will always have children," they said; "they will always replace
you."

Tuhami of course had no children—only women. He continued with an explanation of the origin of the annual pilgrimage. He called it here an *'amara*—a word suggestive of
plenitude—rather than the more usual *musem*.

— People began to visit Sidi 'Ali's tomb every day for three
months and ten days [the mourning period]. The annual pilgrimage first started at this time, when the Sultan Moulay Isma'il

came to visit the tomb. It was then that Sidi Ahmed and his followers began to hit their heads. Lalla Dghughiyya made both men and women fall. When a dancer in the circle of the trance-dance suddenly sees the big eyes of Lalla Dghughiyya, he falls to the ground and enters trance [*jidba*]. There are women who come to watch. Lalla Dghughiyya attracted them and made them dance too.

Lalla Dghughiyya was one of Lalla 'A'isha's many refractions. Tuhami also talked about Lalla 'A'isha Sudaniyya, Lalla 'A'isha Dghugha, Lalla 'A'isha Gnawiyya, Lalla 'A'isha Hasnawiyya, and a host of other female demons who remained nameless or, named, were still identified with the great camel-footed she-demon. Many of these refractions were not recognized by even knowledgeable Hamadsha. Tuhami himself was never particularly clear about them; he often contradicted himself and generally ended up subsuming them all, once more, in 'A'isha Qandisha.

Here is his clearest statement of their relationship:

— Every saint has a Lalla 'A'isha, and they are all different. The most powerful of all is Lalla 'A'isha Sudaniyya at Sidi 'Ali's. She is also called 'A'isha Qandisha. All of the Lalla 'A'ishas form a single family, who live at different saints' [sanctuaries]. Each chooses the saint she likes.

When I asked Tuhami to describe the difference between Lalla 'A'isha and Lalla Dghughiyya, he gave the following confused answer, which I quote in full as an example of his inability to treat the demoness and her refractions coherently. They were symbolically overcharged, resonating, I believe, with all of the women, both real and fictive (if such a distinction can be applied), who peopled his world.

— Lalla 'A'isha chooses good men who are handsome and pious. She pulls them to the center of the dance and forces them to hit their heads. There are times when people in trance have to have bread and olives. One of their friends brings them the bread and olives. The dancer then gives them to those possessed by Lalla 'A'isha. If they do not eat the bread and olives but stash them away in their pockets, they will be corrected by Lalla 'A'isha. She will come to them at night and tickle them—pinch their bones. They will see her in red, white, brown, and light brown. . . .

Tuhami explained that the possessed have to seek the help of a seer and visit 'A'isha's sanctuary in order to appease the demoness. He continued with a stereotypic tale of demonic seduction, this time by another she-demon, Lalla Mira. He had completely forgotten about Lalla Dghughiyya.

— There are times when a man is walking to Sidi Baba [one of Meknes' shantytowns, where Tuhami lived for a time]. A woman comes up to him and asks where he is going. She knows everything about him. He thinks she must be from his home village. . . . It is Lalla Mira or Lalla Malika or Lalla Mimuna. If the man is on good terms with her [if he has done nothing to offend her], nothing happens to him. If he has offended her—if he has gone off with other women—then Lalla Mira goes to Sidi 'Ali. [She can go to all the saints except Moulay Isma'il.] She tells Sidi 'Ali what the man has done. Sidi Ahmed is like a police chief [presumably for Sidi 'Ali]. He commands all the *jnun*. The man becomes sick unless he sleeps with Lalla Mira. When he is asleep, she comes to him in the form of a woman he loves. He sleeps with her, and afterward she visits him often.

Tuhami went on to explain that a man who wants to be rid of Lalla Mira must present his case before a saintly tribunal presided over by Sidi Ahmed.* If the man is patient, Lalla Mira will release him and permit him to marry a woman on her side. Such a woman will appear very beautiful to him. Their children and their children's children (Tuhami did not distinguish here between patrilineal and matrilineal descent) will be on Lalla Mira's side. They will have to wear yellow for her and sponsor an annual trance-dance performed by the Gnawa or Jilala.

— When a man is dressed in yellow, every girl on Lalla Mira's side will be attracted to him even if he is twisted and ugly. Sometimes, if a man comes to a place where Lalla Mira happens to be, she will make him fall down in a fit. She forces him to see a girl he knows and has ignored. If he doesn't pay attention to the girl, she will keep him in the fit. He has to go to the girl when he awakens from the fit. He cannot help himself.

---

*Tuhami's use, here and elsewhere, of legal metaphors to describe the relations that obtain between saints, *jnun*, and humans is not unusual among Moroccans of his background.

Tuhami added that there was a Guerwon* village where everyone wore yellow. Confused, he added that the villagers were all posessed by 'A'isha Qandisha and made an annual pilgrimage to the Hamadsha sanctuaries. In fact, the Guerwon do make such a visit. More than once Tuhami digressed to talk about Lalla 'A'isha. "There are," he said at one point, "also Lalla 'A'isha Franzawiyya, Lalla 'A'isha Inglissiyya . . ." He went on to name a Lalla 'A'isha for each country he could think of; he named Lalla 'A'isha Amerikaniyya with embarrassment.

After Tuhami had described Lalla Mira, as well as Lalla Mimuna and the flirtatious Lalla Malika, who loves perfume and many-colored clothes, I asked again about Lalla Dghughiyya. He had forgotten my initial question.

— She is not a *jinniyya* but a woman from the Gharb. She was Sidi Ahmed's servant. The followers of Sidi Ahmed see her now when they dance the trance-dance. She is the most dangerous of all because Sidi Ahmed is the strongest saint and commands her. She will give an old woman, a seer, cowrie shells. Then Lalla Mira, Lalla Mimuna, Lalla 'A'isha, Lalla Malika, Lalla Khalifiyya, Sidi 'Ali, Sidi Ahmed, Sidi 'Ali Mansur, Sidi Shitani, Sidi 'Ali Sliman at Sidi Sliman Mul-Kifan, Sidi 'Omar Lhasayini, Sidi 'Ali Busarghin, Moulay Bushta, Moulay ben Zahara, Sidi 'Ayed Susi, Sidi Sa'id, Sidi Mohammed ben Qasem, Sidi 'Ali Mnun—they all come to the woman and help her see what is going to happen to the people who visit her.

Tuhami added that such seers have to sponsor a Hamadsha ceremony every year.

— There are some people who hit their heads with stones, jars, braziers, anything that is around. Their blood must flow. If it does not flow, they will not be well. Their blood must flow because Lalla 'A'isha or Lalla Dghughiyya wants it. The blood, it is said, that is on the head of the dancer is also on the head of Lalla 'A'isha or Lalla Dghughiyya. . . . If you have a wound or an ache, you can put a little of the dancer's blood on it and it will get better. You can drink a little of it, too. It all depends on your faith in Allah.

*The Guerwon is a Berber tribe that lives in the Middle Atlas mountains near Meknes.

The most powerful of all the *jinniyya* is Lalla 'A'isha Sudaniyya. . . . There are men who are married to her. You see a beautiful woman. You talk to her about marriage without looking at her feet. If you are clever, the moment you see her, you thrust a steel knife into the ground. Then Lalla 'A'isha disappears. She then says, "Excuse me. Let me go." The man says, "I won't let you go until you promise to give me everything I want." He can ask her not to strike his children, not to take possession of them. He can ask for beautiful clothes. He can ask for a car. He can ask to enter a government minister's office without being seen. Then 'A'isha tells the man what she wants.

(*Tuhami has lost sight of the fact that the man was in total control of the demoness.*)

"I want you to marry me," she says. "But you must not cut your fingernails. You must not cut your hair. Then you will have everything." If the man agrees, he has everything—but it is invisible. What people see is a dirty man with long hair and long fingernails. If the man does not agree (*Tuhami added, catching himself*), then she will leave him alone.

— Why does the man thrust the steel knife into the earth?

— Because she lives in the earth.

— Why doesn't she want him to cut his hair or nails?

— She will be sure of him if he is willing to be dirty like that.

— Can he, can anyone, sleep with her?

— You can sleep with her. You can ejaculate into her just as you can with any woman. You can even have children by her. If you tell anyone, though, you will die.

— Can ordinary people see the children?

— Only Lalla 'A'isha can see her children.

(*Tuhami closed his eyes and was silent for a time. He continued in an abstracted manner.*)

You can see her. She is visible to you, but only to you. She watches you when you make love to your wife. You must make it clear at the time of your marriage to her that you have a wife and want to continue to make love to her. Lalla 'A'isha will permit this.

I was very nervous. There was something uncanny, autonomous, in Tuhami's abstracted manner. I felt as if I were in the presence of someone masturbating. I interrupted him.

— Where is 'A'isha during the trance-dance?

— She is in the center of the circle. You see men drooling. You see them eating bread and olives. You see them eating cactus too. Lalla 'A'isha is watching them, and they are watching her.

Tuhami's manner remained the same, but I was no longer bothered.

— Once I was standing in front of Sidi 'Ali's lodge in the *medina*. I saw a man try to scratch out the eyes of a woman who was standing there. He spit in another man's face, too. He was possessed by Lalla 'A'isha. He did not like—Lalla 'A'isha did not like—the woman. She was against her. Lalla 'A'isha was his alone.

Seduction by a woman leads to control, to enslavement, by a woman. "If Lalla 'A'isha wants a man and if he refuses," Tuhami told me once, "she will tie him up and then make him very thirsty." This theme of enslavement by a woman—the inverse of the articulated standards of male-female relations, of sex and marriage—pervades Moroccan folklore. It is an even more common theme, so to speak, in Tuhami's folklore. My notes are filled with stories of seductions by *jinniyya*s, *ghulat* (female ghouls), and real women. Their names change—usually it is Lalla 'A'isha or one of her refractions—but the story remains the same.

•   •   •

The theme of enslavement is also found in magical beliefs, tales of poisoning and witchcraft, and in the lore of sex and marriage.

— Many Moroccans are poisoned—by women.

— Why?

— To get what they want. There are women who have no money and poison their husbands to get their money.

— What can the husband do?

— Poisoned people never know they are poisoned. They think they are just sick.

— How do they find out?

— There are people who can tell them because they themselves have been poisoned; they can see it in others.

— Are there men who poison?

— No.* Only women. It is only women who do stupid things. God will forget them, the women, on Judgment Day.

— Can a saint help someone who is poisoned?

— That is a question of belief. If a person has faith in a saint, he can visit the saint. The saint might come down to him at night and show him what to do.

— Can Lalla 'A'isha help?

— No. People who are with the demons [*mwali l-ariah*] are never poisoned. . . . There are a lot of poisoners. A man goes off with a lot of women. His wife is jealous. She goes to an *'aguza* [witch] to ask for help. At night the *'aguza* and the woman open the grave of an unknown man. They take a little earth from the grave and mix it with couscous. They must pick up the earth with the corpse's hand. Then the *'aguza* runs around with the hand between her legs. The moon is always red when this happens. Men who know about this run to the cemetery; they chew out the women. Then nothing will happen. If the women are not caught, they feed it [the mixture of earth and couscous] to the man. They can even sell two grams [of the mixture] for one hundred *dirham*s! If a man eats it, he will never again have his health. He will become thin and yellow.

— Are there antidotes?

— There are women who know them. But you have to pay a lot. You take, for example, some couscous, *ras l-hanut* [a mixture of spices], barley, and meat of the land turtle—no other meat. The man who is poisoned takes this to the steam bath and eats it there when his body is very hot. He returns home all bundled up and goes to sleep under a lot of blankets. He remains bundled up all night and loses the poison in his sweat. When he wakes up, he finds that all his clothes are stained with a yellow liquid. He has to drink buttermilk and fenugreek [*helba*] also. Mid-morning, he will have diarrhea. Everything in his stomach will come out. His intestines will be white. (You can remove broken glass from the stomach this way, too, but usually you use cayenne pepper instead of fenugreek.) The man must drink buttermilk and fenugreek for forty days.

— Are there other ways of losing poison?

— You can vomit. You drink sewer water and then you vomit.

*Later in the interview, Tuhami admitted that some men do in fact poison.

There are men who drink sewer water every morning. You filter it through cloth first. I drank it once.

— Why?

— I was thirsty. (*Tuhami seemed proud.*) I used to work for a man who drank sewer water every morning. I prepared it for him. You can also use a mixture of wild rue and water to induce vomiting. You can lose poison through your urine too.

— And through semen?

— No. (*Tuhami's answer was hesitant. He had clearly never thought of the possibility.*) Sometimes the seminal fluid gets blocked.

— What happens then?

— The man gets sick. He can no longer urinate. It burns. He cries all the time. To be cured, he must make love to a black woman. She is hotter and can suck out more of the semen with her vagina.

— And if this doesn't work?

— The man must find a woman with hairy legs. Such women are very strong. You can sleep with them ten times in a row.

— And if that doesn't work?

— Then you must use medicines and spices. . . .

— Can you masturbate to be cured?

— No. That is *haram* [taboo]. If you masturbate, it is said that you are sleeping with your mother.

Several years later I came across this proverb in Westermarck's (1930) study of Moroccan folklore. I had assumed it was Tuhami's own fantasy. He frequently quoted proverbs and other standard expressions of folk wisdom.

— What if a woman sucks you with her mouth?

— No. (*Tuhami blanched.*) [Moroccans of his background do not have oral intercourse. They talk about it a lot; they say the French do it all the time.] It is not good to do it. God gave us something on the bottom, so why take it with the mouth? Today there is a choice —especially with women who do not want children.

— Is it done today?

— Yes, especially among Jews. Moroccans like Jews. Jewish girls think Moroccan men are stronger than Jewish men. There are a lot of Moroccan men who would marry Jewish girls if it were not for their religion.

[Legally a Muslim man can marry a Jewess, but a Muslim woman cannot marry a Jew.]

— Have you ever slept with a Jewish girl?

— No. How much oil would I have to pay?

— I don't understand.

— There is a saying: After you sleep with a Jewish girl, you have to wash with eighty liters of oil before you are clean enough to pray. Or you have to walk down a main street naked. You can sleep with a Christian and eat with a Jew. But not the opposite.

— How does the semen get blocked?

— You can get *l-berd* from going to the baths and leaning against a cold wall. Or from working with your back naked. Or from jumping into cold water when you are hot.

[*L-berd*, literally "the cold," refers to gonorrhea and other venereal diseases. Tuhami had lost the association with poisoning.]

— Can *l-berd* make you impotent?

— Yes.

— What else causes impotence?

— A mother can cause it when she doesn't like the man who hangs around her daughter. She holds a bowl with a top and calls the man. As soon as he answers her, she closes the bowl. She ties it shut and smiles. She can also take a pair of scissors and call the man. As he enters the room, she closes the scissors....

— What can a man do about impotence?

— You have to find out who caused it and then ask her to release you. You may have to promise to do what she wants. Sometimes you can take a little olive oil and put it in a bowl. You lean over the bowl until you can see your penis reflected in the oil. The oil must be clear—no bubbles.

A mother can close her daughter's vagina by turning a hand mill when her daughter answers her call. Then, even if a man tries to sleep with her, he can't. As the mother turns the mill, she says, "Your cry is in the mill."* The mother must open up the stone for her daughter's vagina to open up.

A man should not ejaculate when he deflowers a virgin. Then she will always be too wet. She will be a bog [*merja*].

*The "cry" here refers presumably to the cry of pleasure and pain at the moment of defloration. It may also be associated with the cries of a mother in labor.

Tuhami was referring here to the prevalent belief that leucorrhea results from a man's ejaculating into a woman when he deflowers her. On the wedding night, the groom is supposed to penetrate his bride without ejaculating. What is important is that the hymen break and that the sheet be blood-stained. With typical exaggeration, Tuhami added:

— Even on the second and third night the man should not ejaculate. On the fourth night it is permissible. Otherwise the vagina will become big, and water will flow from it as from a well. There are women who are still dry after you have slept with them ten times. That is good.

(Tuhami now changed the subject abruptly.)

Two weeks ago I went to the movies. I saw a light in the garden when I came home. A few minutes later a man knocked at my door and asked for a room for the night. He came with a woman. I gave them something to eat and then winked at the man and left. When I came back, I found them arguing. The woman wanted ten *dirhams*, and the man wanted to give her five. The lamp fell down and went out. No one could see. I lit a candle, and they continued to argue, with me in the room. I saw that my lamp was broken and that there would soon be a fight. I kicked them out. In the garden the woman said, "Perhaps, seven *dirhams* fifty." I was sure she was married. The man left her. She came back to my house and asked to spend the night with me. "I come from the country," she said. "I'm married. The man picked me up in a car. The driver of the car left us in the field. The man wanted to rape me. By asking him for ten *dirhams*, I knew he would leave me." The woman spent the night with my neighbor's wife. She had come to Meknes to see her sister and had got lost. The next morning I took her to her sister's. I was invited in, but I refused because her sister's husband was a notary. Later she sent me a letter. She invited me to Fez. I went.

Tuhami had forgotten that the woman came from the country. He had not been to Fez in the last two weeks, not even in the last two months. His fantasy became more extravagant, more like an Oriental romance in the movies. He had begun his story by mentioning the movies.

— The woman was waiting for me in a car. There was a chauffeur. She took me to a beautiful house. Her husband was dead.

"I didn't want the other man," she told me, "because I was afraid of getting pregnant. The woman I visited in Meknes was only my breast sister [a woman with whom she had shared her mother's milk]. Tuhami, you must stay here for seven days," she insisted. I spent the night with her, and in the morning I said I was leaving. The woman clapped her hands, and two huge Negroes came in and prevented me from leaving.

Tuhami has personalized the mythic theme of seduction and captivation. He has rendered himself the hero of a romance and has thus effaced himself.

— I stayed until four o'clock, and then I told her I had to go. She still did not want me to go. I told her I wanted to take a walk. She came along. (*Tuhami was getting confused. He could not escape his entrapment.*) I talked to her, and she told me she was sorry she had slept with me. I had been telling her it was *haram* to sleep with a man you were not married to. There is a proverb: If you marry a girl who is not a virgin, she will lead you to wearing a *darbala* [a ragged, patched cloak]. You should not sleep with a girl before you marry her. You should not drink wine with her. You should not go to the movies with her.

There was something incantatorial in Tuhami's voice. Moralism afforded him an escape. He ended his recitation with a story I could not understand fully. A notary refused to marry a couple, saying, "Pimp wants to marry whore." Tuhami in his own story had played something of a pimp's role. He was prepared to supply a room for intercourse and to listen to the negotiations. He had, of course, to maintain his manhood—and lack of manhood—before me and Lhacen.

• • •

— Is it good to take a woman by force?
— No. But a lot of men do it.
— Why?
— Because they have a lot of semen. Such a man cannot talk to a woman. He must have her. This happens when a man hasn't had a woman in a long time. You say that man has a lot of semen and runs with his penis in his hands. He is like a burro. It is the same with a boy of fifteen. . . .

Sexual behavior is autonomous. Tuhami shared this view with
the men of his milieu. Sexual urges in men demand release.
Either physiological reasons are given, as in Tuhami's statement,
or Shitan is held responsible. Women are responsible, too. Intercourse is often described in violent terms. In Meknes slang, the
house where an assignation takes place—Tuhami's room in his
story—is called a slaughterhouse, the penis a knife, the woman a
victim, the act of intercourse a sacrifice. The punishment for
rape is to be forced to marry the woman raped.

— Are there a lot of prostitutes in Meknes?
— Yes.
— How does a woman become a prostitute?
— She puts on makeup and walks around.
— How does she decide to become a prostitute?
— There is a married woman who stays home all day long. She
has a neighbor who is not married. The neighbor visits her,
wearing beautiful silver and even gold jewelry. The woman asks
her where she got all the jewelry. "If only you knew," the neighbor answers. "It was such a splendid place. There was drinking,
such drinks, and beautiful ceilings. . . ." The woman asks herself
what she has been doing with her life. "I'm wasting it," she says.
Then she tells her neighbor that she wants to earn her bread,
too. The neighbor tells her she isn't strong enough sexually. The
woman insists she is strong enough but wants to do it secretly.
"You can't do it secretly," he nieghbor tells her. The woman
finally agrees. The neighbor finds her a rich man. He says he has
never seen such a beauty. The neighbor asks him for ten *dirham*s
for herself. The man takes the woman out. "Now I am beginning
my life," she says. Now the devil has played with her.
— Is it necessary to give every woman money?
— Yes. You should even give your wife something.
— Why?
— Thanks to the woman, you have come. There are men who
have the need and don't have a woman and must pay a prostitute. When you have done this, you think you have done something against religion. You have to go to the baths. It is for
this that you give a woman a little money—for this!

There was something terrifying in Tuhami's cynicism.
I asked Tuhami about ablutions after sexual intercourse. He

explained that if a man—he talked here only of men—did not wash after making love, he would get *l-berd*. He would not be able to say his prayers. He would be polluted. "If you enter a house and it is dirty and smells, you know it is polluted." If a man makes love to his wife, he can work without washing; but if he makes love to another woman, he is too weak to work: "He will sweat a lot and get tired easily; he may even get sick." A man who ejaculates in his sleep is also polluted and has to perform his ablutions.

— This is a big problem for adolescent boys. Then, they are even able to sleep with a donkey! Moroccan blood is very hot, especially around Meknes.
— Why Meknes?
— Moulay Isma'il set the example. Adolescent boys are always looking for women, even old hags.
— And if there are no old hags?
— Then a burro.
— Are there boys who sleep with animals?
— Some go with sheep, some with dogs, others with goats or chickens. (*Tuhami laughed.*)
— Do boys masturbate?
— No.
— Do they go with other boys?
— Yes, with other boys who are smaller or the same age. There is a man here in Meknes—he is seventy—and he still goes with boys. There is another who has three wives and still goes with boys.
— What does a man do when he goes with boys?
— He puts the boy on his stomach and goes deep into his anus—even if the boy faints.
— What is the most polluting act?
— When you have sex with a man.
— Worse than with animals?
— Yes. It is not good to go with men. Look around you.
— Is masturbating polluting?
— That is not permitted. Allah will be very angry. On the Day of Judgment Allah will say: I've given you many beautiful women, but all you can do is use your hand. It is shameful. Allah has given us everything.

Tuhami's attitude toward masturbation is extreme. Although masturbation is considered *haram*, it is accepted as part of the nature of boys (see Pascon and Bentahar, quoted in Marnissi 1975). Adolescent boys will often masturbate by rubbing themselves on each other's buttocks. Anal penetration is not as frequent as Tuhami suggests. Older men do penetrate the boys with whom they sleep. They are looked down on, especially if they do not have intercourse with women too. Older passive male homosexuals are disdained.

Tuhami explained that the only proper way for a man to make love to his wife is in a prone, dominant position. With prostitutes, other positions are possible. (Unlike some of the Moroccan men I questioned, Tuhami did acknowledge the position in which the woman is astride the man. He told me it was called "the vagina over the minaret.") When I asked him why a man can make love to his wife in only one position, he answered, "Allah gave us our wives as he gave us a tree in front of our house. It is to be watered and left alone. Then it will bear fruit." Women—even wives, he admitted—do get pleasure from sexual intercourse.

— They always get pleasure. Their muscles become so relaxed that you could throw them in the ocean and they wouldn't even cry out. All women in the world have only one thought: to make love to a man. At the time of the Prophet, a man could sleep with a woman forty times a night.

Tuhami went on to tell how the Jews worked magic on Sidina 'Ali, the Prophet's son-in-law, and cooled him down and all Muslim men after him. When 'Ali discovered what the Jews had done, he called them to him and massacred them. Blood flowed up to his stirrups. So great was his rage that he would have killed the Muslims too, had not an Arab beggar asked him for a *dirham*. That brought 'Ali to his senses. The Prophet himself is said to have had the sexual vigor of forty men.

— How often do men make love?
— Five or six times a week for the stronger. Then there are others who do it three times, or twice. On Mondays and Thursdays. Thursday is good because you have to wash before going to the mosque anyway.... If a man is strong and has eaten

honey and almonds, butter, and nuts, he can make love five or six times a week. It depends, too, on how old he is.

Tuhami's estimate is far more sober than the estimate I received from other Moroccan men. They talked in terms of five or six times nightly. Some talked even of a self-competition. Semen is believed to come from the blood; a "vein" in the small of the back converts it. Some men told stories of other men, always other men, who made love so many times in a night—fifteen or more—that their vein could not keep up with them and they ejaculated blood.

— Is there anything to do about diminishing sexual powers?

— No. There are people in the markets who sell things, but they are worthless. A man who is accompanied by Shitan can make love all the time. There are women who are always complaining that their husbands don't make love to them anymore.

Tuhami ended the interview with a complicated story in which he helped a woman get her husband back. The husband had been seeing other women and didn't care about her. He only beat her. Tuhami and the woman pushed him into the bedroom; the woman followed, and then Tuhami locked the door on them and refused to open it until the woman called out that it was all right. Tuhami told the woman to give her husband a mixture of butter, cumin, pepper, eggs, cayenne, and beets each morning. They have been happy ever since.

* * *

— A man cannot know if the woman he is making love to will conceive. The woman can tell. She feels it. She feels the child moving in her. The woman's stomach burns a little the night she is impregnated. She can be certain only after three days. She is always tired. She begins to hate her husband a month later. She gets angry at him and tries to scratch his face. She wants special foods: chicken and mutton. She always looks at what her husband has brought from the market. After three months she no longer wants special foods. There are women who make a lot of demands and refuse everything. Some women look at monkeys or pigs when they are pregnant; then their children—their faces only—will look like the animal.

— How is a baby made?

— The male child is always on the right. The girl is always on the left. The girl in the mother's womb sees everything. She sees her father making love to her mother. The boy does not see. The boy turns to his side when his father makes love to his mother. The boy has already learned to be polite by the time he is born. A girl is always curious.

— Where does the child come from?

— When a man and a woman make love, a liquid comes out of the man and enters the woman. It is from this liquid that the child grows. God has made the liquid. When the liquid enters the womb of the woman, the angels take care of it. They stretch it a little bit each month. Then God tells them to leave. The child is like a seed. The seed swells. You can say that it, the child, has been planted in the earth.

— What does the woman contribute?

— There is a pocket in her that stretches.

— Does the woman give anything to the child?

— The child is already there in the man's liquid, but not in the shape of a child. On a night when a woman becomes more excited than usual, you can be sure she will become pregnant. They have been given a child because the angels on each side of them have reported to Allah that they have been good. The angels take a little of what the mother eats and gives it to the child.

Tuhami was referring to the two angels that sit on a man's or a woman's shoulders and keep count of their good and bad deeds. He did not understand my question. For Moroccans of his background, as for the ancient Greeks, the man is wholly responsible for the creation of a child. "The woman you call the mother of the child is not the parent, just a nurse to the seed, the new-sown seed that grows inside her," says Apollo in the *Eumenides* (Aeschylus, 1959 ed.) "The man is the source of life—the one who mounts. She, like a stranger for a stranger, keeps the shoot alive." Such a theory of conception reflects the strongly patrilineal organization of the Moroccan Arab. Women, however, are held responsible for childlessness. When I pointed out a possible contradiction here, Tuhami grew confused. He said that men are responsible for a childless marriage and then that women are. They are unable to receive the man's seed.

— There are women who can't have children because they were poisoned when they were virgins. There are women who cut a little of their hair and bury it in an unmarked grave. Then they will never be able to have children. Also, a woman can take the glass a bride has drunk from on her wedding night and hide it. The bride will not be able to have children until the glass has been found. It is always women who cause barrenness in other women. They are always jealous. They are called the forgotten ones because Allah will forget about them when they are in Paradise. They think only of their vaginas—never about anything else. They never think of death but only of love. This is also true of European women who are not faithful to their husbands. . . .

When a woman is pregnant, she can put her child to sleep. She sees things she does not like: her stomach gets tight, and her child falls asleep. There are special spices she can use to keep the child asleep. She can go into the garden and look at a small olive tree for a while. Then she takes small olives from the tree and burns them until they are almost charcoal. She powders the charred olives, mixes the powder with bread, and eats it.

— Why do women put a child to sleep?

— So they can make love to other men when their husbands are away. Or before they are married.

Tuhami knew of no special diets for women during pregnancy. He knew that women could prevent pregnancies and that by visiting the grotto of 'A'isha Qandisha near Sidi 'Ali's sanctuary—and other special sanctuaries—they could become pregnant. He had no idea whatsoever of fertility periods. Menstrual fluids were very polluting. To make love to a woman during her period caused *l-berd*. Premature births and miscarriages were in the will of Allah. Monsters resulted from American drugs; dwarfs and hunchbacks, from a pregnant woman scratching herself when she wanted a special food. A husband, however, was responsible for meeting his pregnant wife's cravings for special foods. Cauls brought good luck. Like them, the placenta and the umbilical cord could be used in magic. Women began to menstruate only after Eve (Hawwa) ate the forbidden apple in Paradise.

— Iblis* went into Paradise and told Eve that Adam had another woman. Eve did not believe Iblis and wanted to see the woman. Iblis gave her a mirror and told her the woman she saw in the mirror was Adam's other woman. Eve then gave Adam the apple to eat.

Neither of them had anuses until then. (*Tuhami added this as an afterthought.*) And Eve did not have a vagina. After they ate the apple, Adam got an anus and Eve got an anus, a vagina, and her period. (*Tuhami made no mention of Adam's penis.*)†

·   ·   ·

The theme of seduction and captivation requires more than expression in legend or in the lore of sex and marriage. It must be personalized. The Oriental romance with which Tuhami interrupted our discussion about sex was an attempt at personalization. He may have found the discussion embarrassing, anxiety-provoking, fearsome, or simply boring. It was perhaps too abstract, too distant, for him. He was not satisfied, to use Andras Zempleni's (1977) expression, with occupying the comfortable place that the ethnologist's imagination offered him. He was not satisfied with the "neuter pronoun" that I demanded as the result of my reluctance to ask, even my embarrassment in asking him, directly about his own sexual life. Perhaps I did not hear his cry for personal recognition. I was more comfortable in the collective idiom, and I induced him—to what extent I cannot say—to speak in that idiom. Still, he resisted personalization. He, too, showed reticence. Was it for my sake? Or his own? Indeed, was his fear nothing but my (analytic) presumption? I can only suggest that Tuhami himself was neither satisfied with the collective idiom—and the neuter pronoun—nor discontented with it. It had its advantages. Tuhami's tales of saints and demons became personal, but never too personal, until our last meetings, when I knew, and he sensed, that an abrupt ending, the functional equivalent of death within our dialogue, was near.

— Do men like women to let down their hair when they make love?

*Iblis is another word for Satan. It is derived from the Greek *diabolos.*
†See Dwyer (1978), pp. 44–46, for other Moroccan stories of Adam and Eve.

— Married women shouldn't. They should hide their hair a little from their husbands. It is *haram* to show your hair. Only prostitutes show their hair. (*Tuhami made a gesture of utter contempt.*) Some men like it down. Some do not. There are men who ask the whores to undo their hair and take off all their clothes. Then they drink tea and leave without making love.

— Why?

— Because they find their wives prettier. Then there are men who ask a woman again and again to let them sleep with her. She keeps refusing. Finally, when she agrees, the man tells her to take off all her clothes. They have tea and even eat sweets. Then the man says good-bye. That is to get back at her.

— Have you ever done this? (*Tuhami did not seem the least embarrassed by my direct question.*)

— I did it this week. With a woman in Sidi Baba. Her husband is in prison. She knows me well and has often invited me to her house. I kept putting it off. Last Thursday I went to visit her. Her neighbor was there too. We ate together. The woman asked for one hundred francs. I said I didn't have it. She jumped on me to look in my pockets. I had brought a little clay bowl. When I was about to leave, I asked her if she wanted to buy it. "Don't you want to give it to me?" she asked. "Or maybe I can pay you with something besides money." I told her I'd just leave the bowl. I got up and walked to the door. The woman followed me and took me by the shoulders and led me to her room. She told me to sit down and to talk to her some more. She let down her hair and took off all her clothes. Her neighbor took off her clothes too, but she left her hair up. They sat on either side of me and began to flirt with me. I told them to stop. I told the neighbor to leave and told the woman to sleep next to her own children. They again asked me for one hundred francs. I showed them I had none. Then they tried to drag me down. "Pull me," I said, "You're not going to harm me..." To hurt them, I said, "If I don't have a big fat woman, I don't want to sleep with her. She has to be two meters tall!" I didn't want to make love and then have to say prayers the next morning. In the past, if a man did not make love to a woman when she asked him, he was not a man.

Prayer provides Tuhami with an excuse for not living up to the expected standards of male behavior. He is ambivalent, though; he acknowledges that his behavior is not in accord with tradition.

— I left the house. The women asked me to come back for breakfast. They gave me soap and a towel for the baths. I went back to my room and did not return. The next night I went to bed alone and dreamed the neighbor was sleeping in the corner of my room. "Why are you asleep in the corner?" I asked her in the dream.

Tuhami was usually not so careful to differentiate the waking world from the world of dreams. His tone had changed since I asked him directly about lovemaking. He was more "realistically" oriented.

— She asked me to help her lift a chest of drawers. When I tried to help her, she bit me in the neck with her teeth. I asked her why she did this. "I did it because you refused me yesterday. The next time, my bite will be still harder." I woke up. "Oh, that's a problem," I said to myself. "To dream of her all the time!" I left the house. One of my neighbors, a woman, was in front of my door. When women know a man spends a lot of money on them, they follow him all the time. They like a man who talks all the time and makes jokes. . . .

Talking and joking are Tuhami's substitute for money; he gave no woman money. At the end of his recitation he again blends dream and reality:

— Did you ejaculate in your sleep that night?
— No.
— Have you ever?
— No. I never have. If I want a woman, I must have her even if she refuses. In the end, she'll accept. I worked for a European once. His wife was Spanish. She asked me many times. I always refused. A man must be a man. I prefer women who are not married.

Tuhami's tone had changed. It was violent. He always considered Mme Jolan Spanish.

•   •   •

Later in the same interview I asked Tuhami if he had ever experienced the *hal* in his everyday life. The word *hal* refers to the lighter—preliminary—somnambulistic trance into which the Hamadsha fall in their dancing. *Hal* is used also for "weather," "time," and "condition." Among the Moroccans of Tuhami's milieu, it may refer to any state of transport, absentmindedness, or abstraction. A man who is in trance is said, however, to be "out of his conditions," *kharj l-ahawal;* he is said to be absent (*ghaib*).

— When I was little, I didn't do much of anything. I used to spend the night in a cemetery or near a spring. I was like that for two or three years. Then one day I spent the night at the sanctuary of Sidi Sa'id, and the next day I began to work on a farm. I stopped walking around all the time. I got better. At that time my clothers were always torn. During those three years I bought only one new shirt! That was all.

I repeated my question. I did not think that Tuhami had understood it. I did not realize his extension of the meaning of *hal*. Tuhami was referring to his "life in the cemeteries" that had followed his departure from the Jolan family. His emphasis on dirty clothes brings to mind 'A'isha Qandisha's demands on her husbands.

— My body was always very tired. I could hardly get up. I walked a little, stopped, and thought deeply. Then I would make a gesture (*he indicates a gesture of utter resignation*) and walk on slowly.
— What did you think about?
— I thought that all men worked and earned a living and that I did nothing and earned nothing and yet was known by everyone.
— Why did you spend your nights in the cemetery?
— I had no money. What could I do?

I could not bring myself to ask him why he had chosen the cemetery instead of the other places that most of the poor usually chose. Since he seemed much more "realistic" than usual, I tried to establish the chronology of events.

— When did this happen?

— About sixteen years ago.

— What were you doing just before all of this?

— I was in the hospital, and then I worked for Mme Jolan. Her son kept telling me that I ate with them and did nothing. He kept telling me to leave. So I did. I went to Mme Jolan's pay clerk and got my money and left.

Tuhami here gave yet another version of his departure. Each version seemed to account for a specific side of his essentially ambivalent desires for independence, for Mme Jolan, for overcoming her son. Never, however, was there any reference to M. Jolan.

— Did you work for Mme Jolan after your travels?

— I worked for her for two days. I was sick for four. On the fifth day there were the *événements* of Independence.

Tuhami was referring to the violence in Meknes immediately after Independence. A number of *colons* were murdered, several women were raped, and at least one pregnant French woman was disemboweled and her fetus paraded on the tip of a bayonet. A few months earlier, against the advice of his compatriots, the resident general, Grandval, had attempted to talk to a crowd of Moroccans gathered in the principal square of the *medina*. He was forced to shoot his way out. The incident was never forgotten, perhaps because it was one of the few such incidents that accompanied a generally peaceful transition. Many Moroccans claim that it was really refugees from Algeria who were responsible for the violence in Meknes.

— I quit working. People burned down Mme Jolan's house. Her son was the cause. He had taken a machine gun and killed four women. A Moroccan man got into the house and beat him up. Then he pulled him out and burned him. They also burned his father, in the stables. Mme Jolan and her daughters and her youngest son, Antoine, were taken to the Governor's Palace.

— Where were you during all of this?

— I was in my room across the road, where I live now. I had been sick for two weeks. It was lucky I couldn't leave my room. Otherwise I would have been killed.

— Why?

— I would have been next to Mme Jolan's husband. I could
have forewarned them. Sixteen days earlier, I dreamed there
would be a lot of soldiers around the house. I told my boss
something was going to happen in several days. I told him the
dream. One Moroccan killed twelve legionnaires all by himself.
— Why did they attack the Jolan family?
— It was the son's fault. There were a lot of people milling
about, and he fired. People were shouting: "Long live the King!
Down with the French!"
— Was the Jolan house the first to be attacked?
— No. They began in a village near Meknes.
— What did you think when you heard of the son's death?
— I didn't like it. (*Tuhami's face was frozen.*)
— And Mme Jolan's husband?
— The same. Especially for him. He had done nothing. He
had always said that his son was no good and would make
trouble. He was right. M. Jolan and Mme Jolan wanted to be
Muslims, but their son was no good and didn't want them to be.
— Did you ever see Mme Jolan again?
— No. She left for France. Now her factory is rented.

Tuhami grew very quiet. The thought that Mme Jolan also
had been killed kept running through my mind. She had, in fact,
survived, as I discovered later from a French family still living in
Meknes. I was troubled by the thought that Tuhami might not
have been in his room, after all, during these *événements*. I
changed the subject.

— Were you ever afraid when you were little?
— I've been told that certain places are dangerous. I go there,
and I'm never afraid. I've never been afraid except at Sidi
Bushkelet's when a man dressed in white came up to me. The
man took me by my mouth and asked if I wanted to be his son. I
screamed, "Let go." I elbowed him in the stomach. It was soft,
very soft. I screamed. People came. The following morning I
followed his footprints to the cemetery. I thought he might live
there.
(*I could not tell whether Tuhami was reporting a real event or a
dream.*)
— When did this happen?
— I was fourteen. I was on the road to Moulay Idriss's village.

The man was a Hamdushi. There was a large olive tree there.
— Why did the man attack you?
— I don't know.
— Did he want you sexually?
— No. He was a big man. I saw him ford a river. He was big. I
had crossed the bridge, and the man attacked me. Then he
crossed the river. I had been walking and singing.
— Was he ever caught?
— No.
— Who do you think he was?
— Perhaps he was an *'afrit* [a giant *jinn* endowed with extraor-
dinary strength and, in the opinion of some, with seven heads].
Or a *jinn*. I've never seen any others like him. I went to Sidi
'Ali and put in a claim against him. Sidi 'Ali called Sidi Ahmed.
I was asleep and dreamed that Sidi Bushkelet called me. I went to
Sidi Bushkelet's shrine on a Saturday and spent the day. I walked
back home from there in less than a half-hour. I was fasting.
— Were you sick afterwards?
— No. I dreamed that Sidi 'Ali asked me if I knew the man. I
said no. He was big and had a white dress. They looked for him
and couldn't find him. Then Sidi Ahmed found him at Moulay
Bushta's and told me to go to Moulay Idriss's. I went there. The
man in white came and told me he wanted me to be his son. Sidi
'Ali and Sidi Ahmed agreed. Now I'm always with him. If I go to
the *musem* at Moulay Idriss's, I may see him. He is a pious man.
(*I must have looked puzzled.*)
— Have you talked to him?
— I never see his face. I see only his body. He always wears a
jallaba and slippers. He told me I would never see his face until I
married. "Then our eyes will meet," he said. Each time I decide
to marry a virgin or a woman, this man says she's not for me.
— Always? During the night?
— Only during the night.
— During dreams?
— Yes.
— What is his name?
— I don't know.
— What is he—an *'afrit*, a *jinn*, or what?
— I thought he was. But now I know he says his prayers. I
know he is a man like all men.

— Does he protect you?

— No. When he sees that I am depressed, he tells me to visit a friend or go to the movies. I go where he says and talk and feel better.

— Then he is good?

— Yes.

Tuhami was talking himself out of the frightening experience with the man in white. He had never mentioned this "man" before.

— I have this man and another, who is where I work. He is the master of the place [*mul el-blasa*]. He is like the boss. He doesn't want me to play around with women. He wants me to stay alone or go to the movies.

Tuhami slipped and referred to this second man with a feminine pronoun. The *mul el-blasa* is a tutelary spirit similar to the ancient Roman *penates*.

— He doesn't want me to have trouble with my boss. I'm always insulting my boss. Then at night he comes. The boss doesn't say much to me, but I'm always insulting him, and he always leaves in a rage.

It was not clear whether Tuhami was talking about his real boss or about the *mul el-blasa*.

— But he always comes back friendly. Once he came to my room, and he saw a photo. "Son-of-a-bitch, you have a photo—and I don't even have one." [I had promised Tuhami's boss a photo.]

Even if I do nothing, he gives me money. Each year, for five months, I don't work. It is too cold. I can't touch the water to make the tiles. I spend my time selling chick-peas and candies in front of a school. I gossip with the boys and girls. The girls always ask me to give them chick-peas. At the end of the day I have no money.

Two weeks ago I was in Fez. My boss and I had gone to get sand. We saw two girls dressed like Americans, like Egyptians. "I like girls like that," my boss said. "Let's take them to eat something." I talked to them. My boss kept signaling me to bring them back. I asked the girls what they were doing. "Walking," they said. "There is a car," I said. They came with me and got into the truck. The boss bought a kilo of meat, and the girls said they would cook it for us. "We'll show you where we live, and you can come over later," they said. When we went in, later, we found the house was cool. They had prepared a *tajin*. "We don't like Meknes anymore," we said. After we had eaten, they asked us if we wanted to go to sleep. *(Tuhami laughed nervously.)* My boss looked at me. "Why don't you answer?" he asked. He wanted to talk but couldn't. He wanted to know which girl I wanted. I told him it didn't matter. The boss and one of the girls went into another room. She took off her clothes. The other girl asked me if I wanted to go into the other room too. I told her my stomach was full and that I wanted to wait. She put her head against my shoulders. Then she went into the other room and prepared it. I came in and pretended to be asleep. She got undressed. She didn't even have her pants on. She lay down next to me and opened my fly. I slept with her. "It's been a long time since I've seen you," she said afterward. I asked her how she knew me. "I'm not an *'afrit*," I said. "I'm not from around here. I'm from Meknes." She asked me to stay, and I said it was up to the boss. He yelled out. "It's sure. We'll spend the night." My boss wanted to give them thirty *dirham*s, but they refused. They showed us a cabinet filled with gold. When we got back to Meknes, my boss said he would never take me anywhere again. He was afraid the girls would kill him. He wasn't able to make love for eight days. His girl had wrapped her legs so tightly around him that she had hurt his back. He had not been on a bed but on a couch. In the past, the girls from Fez used to lock men in a room and sleep with them until they were all used up.

Tuhami paused. His recitation had clearly relieved him of his depression—diverted him, perhaps, from a reality that was intolerable. Its theme, however, was still another repetition of his seduction and captivation by a woman. The man, at first dangerous, was converted to a saint and then to his boss. Finally, he was the victim of a woman—as Tuhami was.

Our interview had gone well beyond its usual three-hour limit. I decided to insist:

— Who is the *mul el-blasa?*
— He is always with me.
— Does he talk to you?
— Every time I close my eyes.

— Do you have to close your eyes?

— Yes. I want him to tell me I'm free. When I go to the *musem*, I want to be free to marry.

[Tuhami was referring to the annual pilgrimage to Moulay Idriss's sanctuary, which was to take place at the end of August and the beginning of September.]

— When did you meet him?

— When I began to work at the Moroccan's factory. After I left the Jolan's factory.

— Can you see his face?

(Tuhami closed his eyes.)

— I can see his face.

— What does he look like?

— He is white. He is called ben Salam. That is the name of the factory owner.

— Do you ever see him in fact?

— No. Only when I close my eyes or when I'm asleep.

— How did you meet him?

— When I left Mme Jolan. I slept alone. I got to know him a year later.

— Is he a *jinn?*

— No.

— Is he a human being?

— Yes, he is.

— Is there anything you can do about him?

— No. I've tried to leave and find work with someone else, but I can never get work anywhere else.

— Can the other "man" help you?

— They are friends.

— Have you talked to him about Lalla 'A'isha?

— I used to be with her. But now she is nothing to me. She used to bother me a lot, but now it is all right between us.

— Did you do anything to bring this about?

— I fought her sometimes. In the past I had Lalla Malika, Lalla Mira, and Lalla 'A'isha.

— Have they given you peace now?

— Yes.

— Since the arrival of the man?

— No. A year ago they left me after I had gone to Ouazzane to Moulay 'Abdullah Sherif's sanctuary.

— Is it necessary to wait for the men to leave?

— We'll see at the *musem*. Either they will leave me or they will stay with me. God willing, they will leave me.

Tuhami explained, finally, that he had sought help from both a magician-teacher and a seer but that neither had been able to help him.

•   •   •

A few days later I saw Tuhami running across the fields in the direction of the village of Moulay Idriss. I was driving there to watch the preparations for the *musem*. I called to Tuhami and asked if he wanted a ride. He did, but he did not seem to recognize me or my wife or Lhacen; he hardly said a word in the car. He seemed in a daze, in a sort of fugue, really. On the way we stopped at Sidi 'Ali's sanctuary. Tuhami went off to 'A'isha's grotto. He did not go to the saint's tomb itself. We were all puzzled by his behavior, and, when he returned, we asked him if anything was the matter. He said no—as though he were talking to strangers. We left him in the village; he was going to spend the night in the sanctuary.

•   •   •

When I saw Tuhami again, he seemed his old self. Over a month had passed. I had been busy at the *musem* and with other Moroccans. I was beginning to feel the pressure of time. I asked Tuhami if he were supported by a saint. Some Moroccans feel especially close to and protected by a particular saint; they call themselves "followers" of the saint and say they are supported, *msannad,* by him. Tuhami answered that he was supported by Moulay Idriss and gave a long and confusing account of earlier pilgrimages that had finally led to his receiving the saint's support. Significantly, he began his explanation with the return of the King Mohammed V from exile in Madagascar. The French had exiled the king in 1952. His popularity was so great that they were forced to return him to Morocco four years later.

— People were saying the king would come back, but I said he would never come back. One night I saw a man with a pick in

front of a sanctuary. The man with the pick was called Sidi
Mohammed. Next to him stood a woman called 'A'isha. She was
holding a he-goat in her hands. There was another woman next
to him; she had prayer beads. I asked them where they came
from. They answered that they had come from the South. "You
do not know us," they said. Then they told me to bow down to
them. In the morning I got up and said my prayers. The people
kept saying the king would come, and I cried out that it would be
on Tuesday. It was very hot. There were a lot of soldiers around.
An officer told me I was crazy to shout like that, that I would be
thrown in prison. That night I dreamed that a man came from
Moulay Idriss's on a bicycle. I met him on the road, near where
you picked me up in the car a few weeks ago. (*I was surprised that
Tuhami remembered this.*) The man greeted me. I greeted him. He
asked if I recognized him. I said I didn't He asked where I was
going. I answered that I was just going for a walk. He told me to
go to Hamma.

Tuhami did not know where Hamma was. He asked a Buhali,
a member of a wandering mendicant Hedawa brotherhood; the
Buhala are notorious for smoking *kif* and hashish and are reputed for their gift of prophecy. The Buhali told Tuhami to go on
foot, and by the main road, to Moulay Idriss's sanctuary. A week
later, he walked there; his feet were exhausted when he arrived.
There, on the road to the Roman ruins of Volubilis (locally
called the "Pharaoh's Palace"), he saw a spring. It was called
Hamma.

— My head began to swim. I washed my face and fell asleep
next to the spring. I stayed there for three days, sleeping. I ate
nothing. I drank only the springwater. On the third day a man
came and told me I could leave. Only then did I want to leave.
My left foot was all right, but my right foot was still asleep. A
sherif came by. His name was Sidi 'Abderrahman. He told me to
say good-bye, and then I was able to leave.

Tuhami went on to Sidi 'Ali's village. He was led there by a
man in black, who disappeared as soon as they arrived there.
Tuhami did not know where he was. He asked two women; they
told him and fed him couscous. He spent the night in the sanctuary, and on the following morning the two women told him to

go to see Sidi Ahmed. He then listed five other saints whom he
visited.

I did not think Tuhami had understood my question about
how he had become a follower of Moulay Idriss. I repeated it.
He answered this time, that he had not chosen the saint but that
the saint had chosen him.

— It was at the time of the Feast of the Sheep ['Ayd l-Kebir]. I
was told that those who wanted to make a pilgrimage to Mecca
had to visit Moulay Idriss's shrine nine days after the feast. I did
not believe this. I dreamed that a man gave me a white candle.
"What can I do with this?" I asked. "You must bring it to me," he
answered. At two the next afternoon I took the road to the
village of Moulay Idriss. I spent the night in the sanctuary,
praying. I found 750 francs at the entrance. A man told me to
take it.

The man in the dream—and the man who told him to take the
money—was Moulay Idriss. Finding the money was a sign of his
support. It is likely that the man on the bicycle in the earlier
dream was also Moulay Idriss.

At the time, I did not understand that, by recounting his many
pilgrimages, Tuhami was underscoring the importance of
Moulay Idriss as a fixed point, an orientation point, in his life.
Or, given the importance he had bestowed on the saint in our
last meeting, he was perhaps creating that function for the saint.
He had not mentioned Moulay Idriss very often in our previous
talks. In both accounts Moulay Idriss is of significance only after
Tuhami has transgressed: first by not supporting, and then by
publicly supporting, the king and, later, by refusing to recognize
the necessity of visiting the saint's sanctuary before attempting a
pilgrimage to Mecca.

Tuhami often mentioned his desire to make the pilgrimage to
Mecca and bemoaned the fact that he would never have enough
money. The pilgrimage to Mecca is one of the five duties of all
Muslims. Mecca is considered to be the center, the navel, of the
world, and the sanctuary of Moulay Idriss is symbolically associated with it by many Moroccans. They say that the spring of
Zemsma at his sanctuary is connected with the spring of Zemzem
at Mecca by an underground stream. Tuhami's change of mind
over the return of the king may reflect a certain ambivalence he

felt about Moroccan Independence. With it came the death of M. Jolan and his son and the flight of Mme Jolan and her daughters. (Many Moroccans of his milieu were sorry to see the French leave; they missed the sense of stability the French gave them. "Independence came fifty years too early," Tuhami once told me.) The two women—one with a he-goat, a sacrificial victim; the other with prayer beads—are perhaps symbolic of the two aspects of women in Tuhami's experience; they are reduplicated in his arrival at Sidi 'Ali's village. One—her name is 'A'isha—represents the side symbolized by the female *jnun;* the other, nameless, represents the other side of women, which Tuhami is unable to articulate. His idiom affords him no image, no name, for her. I am tempted to identify her with the more transcendental, the more quietly mystical, the less chthonic side of his belief—with the Ahl Twat, the Wazzana, rather than the Hamadsha. Women do not use prayer beads. Both 'A'isha and her nameless companion offer two modes of salvation. Significantly, they flank a man named Sidi Mohammed. Both the Prophet and the king bore this name.

I asked Tuhami if he had ever found himself far from home without knowing how he got there. I was certain I had found him in a fugue that day on the way to the village of Moulay Idriss.

— Yes. Several times. Once I found myself in El Hajeb [a Berber town about twenty miles from Meknes]. I left my meal cooking. I returned to Meknes on foot, laughing. My boss asked where I had been. I said I had been near the movies. I used to make long trips without telling him. When people asked me where I had been, I told them it was none of their business.

Tuhami then told me about a girl from Taza who lived in Meknes. Her father wrote to her, saying that her mother had died and that he wanted her to come back home to Taza. Tuhami didn't want her to leave. He dreamed that her mother had not died, that her father only wanted her to return to buy him wine and *kif.* He told her the dream, and she wrote back to her father saying that she knew her mother was alive. In the dream, Tuhami saw her father—he was a *qa'id,* a judge—flanked by two girls. The *qa'id* said that the girls would have to leave, now that Tuhami had arrived. One of the girls touched Tuhami with her shoulder. "Don't touch me," Tuhami told her, "or I will get angry."

Again the image of the two women and a man. Tuhami's presence will force them to leave. One of the women angers him: she touches his shoulder. He had the dream—he himself admitted this—because he did not want the girl from Taza to leave. He liked her. Did he feel that his desire tainted him? The man this time is transformed from *qa'id* to drunk and addict.

— Do you remember what happened before you went to El Hajeb?

— I was just working. I was in the sun. The boss's brother and I were talking. He suggested we go to the movies or to the whores. I thought I was with him all the time, and then I found myself alone in El-Hajeb. I was barefooted.

Dreams, recitations, pilgrimages, moralism, even fugue—they all served to protect him from sexual encounters.

— Have you ever suffered a loss of memory?

— I forget a lot. I walk, and suddenly I ask myself why I am where I am. I don't know. When you picked me up that day I didn't know what I was doing there. I had been talking to friends. The next thing I remember is your calling me. I was surprised. My mouth was open. I had eaten grapes, and that is why I was sick. After I left you at Sidi 'Ali's sanctuary, I went into 'A'isha's grotto and someone told me not to eat grapes again. He asked me to take a walk, but I refused. He insisted. The man said the female boss was waiting for me. I told Mohammed [a friend who had come with us and had gone to the grotto with Tuhami] to stand by me. He did not understand. Then I was with you, and you didn't know, either, that the man was bumping into me.

Tuhami went on to describe an argument with Mohammed over the exact location of 'A'isha's grotto, The grotto itself is divided into two chambers.

I then asked Tuhami if he was afraid of heights, dogs, closed-in spaces, or wide-open spaces. He said he was not. I then asked him if he was afraid of water.

— No. I've been afraid of rivers ever since I was little. I was a shepherd. My friend fell into the river and was carried away. Since then I've always been afraid of rivers. I was with my friend. He said that, if he ever saw Lalla 'A'isha, he would hit her or throw a rock at her. There was thunder, and suddenly the river swelled and carried him away. We were trying to climb on a mule at the moment, and the mule fell into the river. My friend let go, but I held onto the mule. I didn't know how to swim. I couldn't help him. My parents always said that they would throw me into the river if I ever cried. I was afraid of nothing else.

— What did you do?

— I took the sheep back to the village, all alone, and told my father what had happened. My father gave a *sadaqa* [a feast], with scribes who read from the Koran. I came to Meknes right after that.

— How did you feel when all this happened?

— My head was dry, like a rock. I was mute for two days. Ever since then I have found myself in misery on the road. Some say I'll never marry. All my friends are married except for me.

— Did you ever think that you could have saved him?

— We were both carried away. Neither of us knew how to swim. I could have helped him if the mule had been closer. I couldn't let go. If I had touched my friend, he would have pulled me off and down. If I had been carried away by the river, then all the flock would have been lost.

I took the death of Tuhami's friend to be real, just as Freud took as real the seductions of his female patients by their fathers. I had discovered *the* event that was central to Tuhami, the subject of his persistent metaphorizations, the root of his emptiness, his impotence, his being as dead. I had discovered the "fatal instant," to quote Jean-Paul Sartre (1964) that Tuhami, like Jean Genet, carried in his heart, the instant that had lost none of its virulence, the instant that Tuhami continued to live and relive—the "infinitesimal and sacred void which concludes a death and begins a horrible metamorphosis."

At the time I did not recognize my presumption. I *understood*. I did not realize that Tuhami's recitation was for me symbolic of my own transformation. I committed what Erikson (1969) would call the "sin of originology." Tuhami did continue to speak the language of the "real" with but few lapses into what I took to be the "imaginary."* (His tale of the pasha's son was one such lapse.) I did not then understand that the real was a metaphor for the true—and not identical with it. Tuhami had been speaking the truth from the very start, even in his interviews with Lhacen, but I had been listening only for the real, which I mistook for the true. The truth was for me the real masked by the metaphor. Such was my cultural bias.

I concluded the interview by asking Tuhami if he had ever had swelling sensations (many trancers report this sensation).

— No. Only when I am depressed. My heart swells, and I feel as though my body will explode.

— When did you feel this way last?

— About a month ago. I am poor. I was with my sister. She began to scold me. She kept asking me why I go to whores and saints and never get married. She is always asking me this. Even my neighbors ask the same thing: why I don't get married. It irritates me. It is up to Allah. There is nothing I can do about it.

---

*I am reminded of Gérard de Nerval's struggle in *Les Nuits d'Octobre* (1966 ed.) to write as a realist rather than as a romantic after reading Charles Dickens. There are striking parallels between this French romantic—the author of *Aurélia*, an account of madness, and a historian of Illuminism—and Tuhami. Like Tuhami, Nerval split his women into many refractions—and condensed them into single figures of mysterious ontological status.

Part Four

There had been something desperate in Tuhami's last words: "Even my neighbors ask the same thing: why I don't get married. It irritates me. It is up to Allah. There is nothing I can do about it." I knew that I could no longer maintain ethnographic distance. Tuhami's appeal was too great, and I myself too much of an activist, to accept what I understood then to be his passivity before forces externalized in 'A'isha Qandisha, the saints, and ultimately Allah. I was a doer, and I came from a culture of doers—a culture that could accept as reasonable the maxim "Nothing is impossible." I had learned this maxim as a child, and others like it ("Try, try, and try again; and if at first you don't succeed, try, try again"; "Don't give up the ship"; etc.). I had read modern versions of Horatio Alger and understood self-help and Nietzsche's notion of self-overcoming. I was angered by Tuhami's passivity before the demonic, his fatalism, his submission to Allah's will, to what was "written." His beliefs, I was convinced at the moment, held him back; they hindered his self-expression and impeded his self-reliance; they precluded the possibility of self-overcoming. They were a sanctioned ground for rationalization. There was, I realized, a limit to my relativism. I became a curer. I was leaving in two weeks. I was anxious for Tuhami. My wife and I even talked about staying longer, but that was impossible.

I write: "I became a curer." In fact, I had already become a curer. This is evident in my notes, and the reader is certainly aware of the way in which Tuhami and I both negotiated our exchange into a therapeutic one. Tuhami provided me (and I feel the consequence of this even now, as I write) with the possibility for maneuver, manipulation, and cure, with the occasion for a vicarious participation that was perhaps not so vicarious after all. (My own father died when I was young, though not so young as Tuhami had been.) And he provided me with the occasion for that romance of adventure and exploration that was, I imagine, what drew me, and continues to draw me to anthropology and field research. The moment I have cited as marking my change of status is for me one of those fatal instants that mark a moment in what has been recollected and will be repeated. Repetition and recollection, Kierkegaard (1964, p. 33) tells us, "are the same movement, only in opposite directions; for what is recollected has been, is repeated backwards, whereas repetition properly so called is recollected forwards."

"Ethnographic distance" was a rhetorical device that enabled me both to mask my position and to rationalize it. Certainly, as I look back over my meetings with Tuhami, it is clear that the "distance" between us—and the intensity of our involvement— varied considerably, despite even the presence of Lhacen, my field assistant. The methodological strategies of the field worker are, as George Devereux (1967) has observed, frequently the result of his anxieties. Indeed, so, frequently, are his epistemological concerns.

I had arrived in Morocco as a stranger with a determination to understand at least some small facet of the lives of the people that, for whatever reason, I found intriguing and somehow significant. I met many Moroccans whom I found uninteresting and unlikable, and I met some whom I found interesting and unlikable. I was also fortunate enough to meet a few who were both interesting and likable, and Tuhami was among these. He was, within his terms, giving; and I, with an avariciousness supported by my science, was willing to receive. I wanted to possess everything that Tuhami knew and could tell me—and even more. I wanted to know him completely. I have always been fascinated by d'Annunzio's portrayal, in *The Triumph of Death* (1900), of hero and heroine's obsessive desire to know each other fully. The presumption that such knowledge can be achieved rests either on the belief in total sexual possession—a possession that ends up, as d'Annunzio understood, in total extinction—or on the reduction of the Other to that which is completely graspable: the specimen. The one, the goal of passion, and the other, the product of science, are not in fact so easily separable. Both are of course illusory.

"The picture of another man that a man gains through personal contact with him," Georg Simmel observed in 1908, "is based on certain distortions."

These are not simple mistakes resulting from incomplete experience, defective vision, or sympathetic or anti-pathetic prejudices. They are fundamental changes in the quality of the actual object perceived. [Simmel, 1965 ed., p. 342]

These qualitative distortions result, if I understand Simmel correctly, from generalizations in some measure of the Other qua individual.

In order to know a man, we see him not in terms of his pure individuality, but carried, lifted up or lowered, by the general type under which we classify him. Even when this transformation from the singular to the typical is so imperceptible that we cannot recognize it immediately; even when all the characterological concepts such as "moral" or "immoral," "free" or "unfree," "lordly" or "slavish" and so on, clearly appear inadequate, we privately persist in labeling a man according to an unverbalized type, a type which does not coincide with his pure, individual being. [Ibid., p. 343]

These generalizations, which result from our fragmentary knowledge of the Other, both detract and supplement his individuality. The individual is, for Simmel, always in tension with the a priori, operative categories through which he is pictured.* These categories, or typifications, as we would call them today, include, ironically, the "singular individual." Although it might

---

*With respect to the "Orient"—and this would include "Morocco"—these categories or typifications have, as Edward Said (1978) has recently argued, a "discursive consistency" that is embedded in a distinct European and American ideology. The "Oriental," the "Moroccan," "Tuhami" as a type, are all representations in an inevitably distorting language. They are—and here I part company with Said—subject to some partial reformulation in the negotiations that transpire in "lived encounters" with the Oriental, with the Moroccan, with Tuhami. These reformulations are still deformations, to use the jargon; but they do raise the problematic of traditional representations and even give the mutually satisfying illusion of a corrective to these representations. What is sadly lacking in Said's work (and is its pathetic irony) is an encounter with the Oriental in person or text. (There is, after all, a long scholarly tradition in the "Orient" that has profoundly affected the Orientalist's perception and scholarship.) Said's critical and even self-critical stance serves only to relocate him, inevitably, he would argue, in the Orientalist discourse. He, his text, is frozen in the "chosen" moment of an arrested dialectic.

well appear that the apprehension of this singular individual should form the basis for correct relations with the Other, such an apprehension would itself be a distortion of the individual as a social being. The very alterations and new formations that preclude the ideal knowledge of the Other—the qualitative distortions—"are, actually, the conditions which make possible the sort of relations we call social" (ibid., p. 345). "The individual is contained in sociation and, at the same time, finds himself confronted by it" (ibid., p. 350).

I quote Simmel at some length here because, in his roughshod Kantian way, he struggled in his Introduction to *Soziologie: Untersuchungen über die Formen der Vergesellschaftung* with the problem of the knowledge of the Other with a passion and a freshness that have been lost in later theories of labeling, typification, and alienation. His argument, reformulated in hermeneutical terms, is that we come to know another individual with a certain foreknowledge*—a foreknowledge that is sanctioned by social convention (i.e., tradition), that fills in the "incompleteness" of that individual's presentation, and that qualitatively modifies the individual as a subject of perception. Such knowledge, for Simmel, demands similarity, "because we cannot fully represent to ourselves an individuality which deviates from our own" (1965, p. 343). It also demands dissimilarity, "in order to gain distance and objectivity." The knowledge of the Other requires, however paradoxically, both similarity and dissimilarity:

> Nevertheless, *perfect* cognition presupposes perfect identity. It seems, however, that every individual has in himself a core of individuality which cannot be re-created by anybody else whose core differs from his own. And the challenge to re-create is logically incompatible with psychological distance and objective judgment, which are also bases for representing another. [Ibid., p. 343]

Simmel is led to conclude: "We cannot know completely the individuality of another." And this fact, however described, is, I believe, essential to the understanding of all social encounters. It is perhaps no accident that C. G. Jung (1961) concluded his autobiographical meditation with a personal anagram that he

*Or, perhaps more accurately, "fore-understanding" (Gadamer 1960).

left unexplained. It is also no accident that Simmel himself wrote
about the lie and the secret.

In most of our ordinary encounters, the assumptions of similarity and dissimilarity are accepted without question. It is only
in the exceptional encounter that they come into question. And
there are certain moments, but only certain moments, in the
ethnographic encounter when they are indeed questioned. As I
have written earlier, in most social encounters we assume that
what a person says he experienced he did in fact experience; we
assume that we can know another person, at least up to a certain
point; and we assume the transparency of language. Such assumptions are, I believe, mystifications—at least from a strict
epistemological point of view—that are necessary for social
existence. We must assume knowledge not only of the Other as
an external actor—a soulless marionette—but as an experienc-
ing individual with whom we are in as-sociation. We are rarely
pushed, except in the height of romantic passion or in the biographical enterprise, to assume, or even to desire, as Simmel
would put it, "perfect cognition" of the Other. (To be sure, such
perfect cognition occasionally becomes an ideal within those
utopian movements that Victor Turner [1974] has characterized
as *communitas,* but such movements are for the most part
characterized by an extreme psychological naïveté.) The push
toward such cognition—fusion, really—is motivated, I suggest,
by the fear of the very opposite—solipsistic miscognition or
de-fusion—which the psychoanalyst would associate with separation.

The ethnographer's entry into the field is always a separation
from his world of primary reference—the world through which
he obtains, and maintains, his sense of self and his sense of
reality. He is suddenly confronted with the possibility of Otherness, and his immediate response to this Otherness is to seek
both the security of the similar and the distance and objectivity
of the dissimilar. No longer bound to the conventions of similarity and dissimilarity that obtain within this own world of reference, he vacillates between an overemphasis on the similar or on
the dissimilar; at times, especially under stress, he freezes his
relationship with—his understanding of—this Otherness. He
may become overly rigid, and his rigidity may determine the
"texts" he elicits and the form he gives them. He may, in his

anxiety, attempt to arrest time. Fortunately, the field experience is a lived experience that perdures, permitting a certain learning and requiring a flexibility that militates against this tendency to freeze both the relation with, and the understanding of, Otherness. Fortunately, too, most ethnographic encounters are, despite even the ethnographer, very human experiences. The savage is, so to speak, less cowed by the ethnographer than the ethnographer is by the savage.

I came to Morocco with an awareness of Otherness. I had been there briefly as a tourist several years before I began my field study, and I had lived in several other societies that were, in their own ways, more alien to me than Morocco. I did not meet Tuhami until I had been in Meknes for several weeks. He did not immediately threaten my taken-for-granted world. I had already been shocked on more than one occasion into questioning that world. (The most dramatic but hardly the most significant example was the first time I saw a Hamdushi slash his head until he was drenched with blood; the more significant examples were far less dramatic and in their own right hardly memorable: e.g., eating in restaurants in which there were never any women, waiting for hours for a new and casual acquaintance to feed me an enormous meal). I had reached a moment of flexible accommodation with my new Moroccan reality when I first met Tuhami. I could get along.

Such moments of flexible accommodation punctuate the field experience. If there are no conventions for describing encounters between two or more persons, they are quickly negotiated, but in a very specific and superficial manner. They are determined by the most essential matters on hand. With time, however, one's relations deepen and become more complex; they demand new accommodations—and new conventions. As Paul Rabinow observed with respect to his Moroccan informant Ali:

> there began to emerge a mutually constructed ground of experience and understanding, a realm of tenuous common sense which was constantly breaking down, being patched up, and re-examined, first here, then there. [Rabinow 1977, p. 39]

Field work must be understood within its temporal dimension as a process of continual discovery and self-discovery. There is considerable truth in Paul Ricoeur's involuted definition—quoted by Rabinow (1977)—of the hermeneutic as "the comprehension of self by the detours of the comprehension of the other." There is also a value, coordinate with tact and respect for the other, in pushing the swing of comprehension back to the other.

There is no doubt that I learned much about myself and my world through the detour of my comprehension of Tuhami. Some of this I have thought relevant to my study, and I have attempted to convey it explicitly or implicitly. Some of it I find irrelevant—and even irreverent to Tuhami—and I have tried to omit it. I am not, after all, engaged in autobiography, except in the most tenuous sense. I am certainly not interested in confession and expiation, though both confession and expiation enter inevitably into my enterprise.

As I look back over my notes, and as I attempt to recall my meetings with Tuhami some ten years ago, I am immediately struck by the impoverished quality of my emotional response. My questions seem frequently cold, unemotional, and detached. Was I frozen before Tuhami? In part, the question must be answered in the affirmative. There were times when my relations with Tuhami specifically or with Morocco and the Hamadsha more generally—the two cannot easily be distinguished—were such that I could not permit myself any response but the most distant. It was at such times that I took refuge in my difficulties with Arabic and exploited, I suppose, the presence of Lhacen. It was at such times, too, that I made use of "ethnographic distance" and various theoretical positions, most notably the psychoanalytic but others as well, to distance myself and to defend myself from an onslaught of presumably intolerable emotions. (I should add here that Tuhami took refuge at times in Lhacen's presence, in "ethnographic distance" as he understood it, and, undoubtedly, in his own theoretical understanding of what was transpiring.)

Even today, as I write, such defensive maneuvers, in more attenuated form, I believe, come into play. Indeed, at some level, my literary enterprise must be conceived in such terms. I have difficulty, both stylistically and psychologically, in distinguishing the time of encounter from the time of writing. For Tuhami, I have my notes; for myself, I have only my memory. I do not know when my theoretical confabulations, my observations and explications, result immediately from the encounter and when they result from the literary reencounter. I note, for example, that I have tended to overinterpret Tuhami's words in the first pages of his portrait. Is this a result simply of the need to introduce the reader to Tuhami and his culture and to explain my own theoretical orientation? Or am I repeating the over-interpretation that comes in the first months of field work? Am I, in other words, recreating a past response or responding anew to an encounter?

The ethnographic encounter, like any encounter, however distorted in its immediacy or through time, never ends. It continually demands interpretation and accommodation. The ethnography, as I have written elsewhere (Crapanzano 1977d), is an attempt to put a full stop to an encounter that is necessarily disorienting. The same may be said of the portrait, the case history, the life history, the biography, and even the autobiography. In their own ways they all demand a cessation of time—a complete departure from the encounter. The sadness, the guilt, the feelings of solitude, and the love that come with departure and death will not, cannot, end. Tuhami has come to embody these feelings for me, much, I think, as the demons that haunted him embodied similar feelings for him.

There was always something captivating about Tuhami's discourse. It was as though he wanted to entrap me, to enslave me *through the power of the word* in an intricate web of fantasy and reality—to reverse, if you will, the colonial relationship that I as a foreigner, a *nasrani*, must have suggested to him. There was something seductive in his discourse, too. He did not in fact want *me* or anyone else. That would have been too immediate, too burdensome, too demanding for him. What he wanted, I have come to believe, was rather the imaginary fulfillment of an emptiness, a lack, a *manque-à-être,* to use Jacques Lacan's (1966) phrase, that he suffered. I became, I imagine, an articulatory pivot about which he could spin out his fantasies in order to create himself as he desired. I was created to create him, to fill metaphorically the emptiness that his desire, in its perversity, desired. Tuhami wanted fulfillment through the metaphor without denying the essentially irreal quality of the metaphor. Anything more concrete would have been too dangerously real.

As for me, I was soon captivated and seduced by Tuhami's evocations. I now see signs of captivation and seduction in my very first meeting with him. I guarded myself with the devices offered by my science and with a certain forced naïveté. I would return from my sessions with Tuhami filled with the joy of discovery and eagerly describe them to my wife.* We were fascinated and pleased with the constant deepening of our awareness of Morocco that came through Tuhami and many of my other informants. I pushed ever deeper, sometimes without the restraint that is required in such encounters. (Lhacen frequently corrected my haste with his sure sense of tact and his indomitable patience; he too was excited by our discoveries.) Tuhami was, at the beginning and occasionally at other times during our meetings, potentially graspable. All that was required was time. His distance from me, his dissimilarity, made him into a specimen. But I soon felt very uneasy in this attitude. My conversations with my wife soon shifted from fascination and joy to concern and worry. We were coming to know Tuhami as a person and beginning not only to sympathize with his condition but to empathize with him. Care had entered our relationship.

A confident empathy is not readily forthcoming in field work. The field worker is often overwhelmed by dissimilarity; he is too distant and too objective. To experience the Other as a subject through the full range of his emotions, Sartre (1956) observes, is not an act of passive cognition. It is an active granting of importance—importance for oneself—to the Other's subjectivity. The Other must matter in one's own self-constitution; he must not simply be an object of scientific or quasi-scientific scrutiny. To understand the Other, the ethnographer must come to participate as best he can in the Other's reality. Aside from the usual difficulties that come with entering into an alien cultural tradition, the ethnographer is caught within a dilemma of intentionality that has come to be described by the oxymoron "participant observation" (Rabinow 1977). On the one hand, the ethnographer must engage in the life of the people he studies; he must enter into their intentionally determined world—the world of their praxis; and he must permit himself somehow only

---

*My wife had met Tuhami on several occasions, once when Tuhami took us on a tour of the sanctuaries in and around Meknes and again when we came upon him on his way to the shrines of Sidi 'Ali and Moulay Idriss. She did not come to our meetings, but the fact of her existence must have influenced Tuhami's relationship to me. At the time, we were in our late twenties and still childless.

the self-reflection necessitated by their (and his) particular praxis. (I assume here that all intentional activities both demand and delimit self-reflection.) On the other hand, the field worker must remain faithful to his own primary intention: to do research. He must be able to remove himself from the life of the people he studies; he must remain outside their intentionally determined world; and he must permit himself a self-reflection that is demanded and delimited by his own particular praxis, his research.

The instant that marked the change in my relationship with Tuhami reflects, I believe, my own inability to maintain, or to pretend to maintain, these two distinct intentionalities. Tuhami had come to matter to me. My science and even the presence of Lhacen were no longer sufficient to distance me from him. His dissimilarity had fallen away to reveal his similarity. (Or perhaps I had discovered in his dissimilarity a similarity, though I do not think this was the case at the time.) And I believe I had come to matter for him. I see evidence of this not only in his response to me and to Lhacen—and Lhacen's to me, for that matter—but in several of Tuhami's dreams that I report in the next part of this book. Unfortunately, I have no exact record of my own dreams. I do remember, rather vaguely, a dream fragment I had, either toward the end of my stay in Morocco or several seeks later in Paris. I was watching Tuhami, from the outside, sitting cross-legged in the courtyard of a saint's tomb. The tomb itself was brilliantly white. He was wearing very bright blue pants and was swaying back and forth in meditation—oblivious of me. Then (a secondary elaboration, I believe) he looked up and smiled at me.*

This change precluded, at least at the time, the maintenance of a double intentionality. I had to respond to Tuhami in the

---

*I should point out that in Paris, several weeks before my arrival in Morocco, I dreamed anxiously that I was trapped in a saint's tomb—it was white and damp like clay—and that I was rescued by a woman's brown hand that pulled me through a slit-like window. When I first came to Meknes, several Hamadsha, who were still suspicious of me, asked if I had ever dreamed about Morocco. I told them the dream, and they said that it meant that 'A'isha Qandisha had sent for me. One of them a *muqaddim*, began to call me "Tahush"—the name of an important *jinn*, he explained, laughing. My relations with the Hamadsha improved immensely thereafter. Tuhami was not among the Hamadsha and probably never heard of my dream or of my *jinn*-name.

immediacy of our relationship. I was relieved, and so was Lhacen, who, despite his sophistication, must have been puzzled by
the very strange transactions I had initiated. He began to re-
iterate the advice I was giving to Tuhami. I was nervous and at
times stiff in my new role, less because of its newness than because of my imminent departure.

Tuhami was relieved, too. He yielded to me. He came to speak
my language—the language of the "real" rather than the
"imaginary," however sanctioned it was by his traditional idiom.
I was unable at the time to recognize the putative quality of the
real; I did not understand that the "real" as well as the "imaginary" can serve a metaphorical function. The colonial relationship was restored. I was secure and could rationalize my
position as protector-therapist. Tuhami accepted this reversal
with ease, not simply because it is always easier to return to old
ways, especially when dependency is involved, but because he
could at last understand our relationship. Although my ways
were mysterious to him, their mystery itself was familiar. The
ways of the Moroccan curer, like the ways of all curers, are
always mysterious.*

I have been writing largely as though Tuhami and I were
conversing alone. I have ignored Lhacen. In Part One I wrote:

> As a Moroccan and yet a stranger to Meknes, and as a Berber,
> Lhacen provided, I believe, a "familiar distance" that was nec-
> essary for the frankness of our discourse. Had he not been
> there, our relationship would have been awkward. Present, he
> could be ignored and was ignored.

Masked here by a rhetorical flourish is a significant contradiction. How could Lhacen both free the relationship between
Tuhami and me of its awkwardness and yet be ignored? To consider this contradiction—and it must be considered—is to consider the role of the Third in any relationship. Lhacen's presence raises the question of the use of a field assistant or an
interpreter in anthropological research.

---

*I have spoken here as though only the change in *my* attitude was responsible
for the change in our relationship. I have thus preempted the initiative, have
declared Tuhami passive and myself active and free of influence, and have
falsified the dynamics of our relationship. Even the most directed relationships
involve a negotiation of reality by both parties.

In my field work I have worked both alone and with a field assistant. I have found that there is a qualitative difference in the material obtained in the two situations. Contrary to what I would have expected on theoretical grounds, I have found that the material I collected with a field assistant, at least in the initial phases of research, had an intimacy of tone and detail that I did not obtain when I worked alone.

Lhacen—and the field assistant more generally—served to mediate the relationship between Tuhami and me in a very complex manner. He and I were both strangers—to Meknes, to Tuhami, and to each other. I was a stranger to Morocco as well. We shared, in our relationship with Tuhami, that "unity of nearness and remoteness" that Simmel (1964a) finds in the "phenomenon of the stranger." In relationship with the stranger, "distance means that he, who is close by, is far, and strangeness means that he, who is also far, is actually near" (Simmel 1964a, p. 402). As strangers we shared a kind of objectivity (see Schutz 1944; Nash 1963), a detachment even, that was rationalized in my case by my science and in Lhacen's case perhaps by the "job" he was performing for me. We shared a common intention: to learn as much as we could about the Hamadsha and about the people, like Tuhami, around them. In different ways, we were both entrapped in the formulations of that intention. The most significant of these, and for me, at least, the most personally distasteful, was the formulation—the creation—of the informant, whom I frequently confused, and still confuse in my reveries, with the "informer."* Lhacen told me after meeting Tuhami for the first time that he had discovered "un informateur formidable." I was excited by the prospect, but now, in retrospect, I am troubled by it. Tuhami, Moroccans more generally, and the Hamadsha had become for Lhacen, as well as for me, informants-to-be-discovered! Lhacen and I had talked for many hours about Morocco, the Hamadsha, ourselves, and about my research aims and strategies. We had visited many sanctuaries and brotherhoods throughout Morocco

---

*I am not alone among anthropologists and the readers of anthropology in equating the informant with the informer. The confusion results from a guilt-inspiring voyeuristic intention that can be rationalized away no more in the anthropological endeavor (by science) than in the psychoanalytic endeavor (by cure).

before finally deciding on the Hamadsha in and around Meknes. We had rehearsed, so to speak, "our" research. We accommodated ourselves to it, to each other, and to the people, now potential informants, with whom we were to work. We became friends; but in differing ways and for different reasons we cast the eye of a stranger on our relationship to each other. Lhacen was for me always a Moroccan, an informant—privileged to be sure—in his own right. I was his employer, who offered him not only a livelihood but the opportunity to acquire knowledge that could be of potential benefit to him.

Lhacen and I were strangers in very different ways. I was an American, a *nasrani*, a speaker of French—the language of the *colon*—a man of letters. Lhacen was a Berber from Marrakech, originally from an isolated village high in the Atlas Mountains, a *sherif*, a member of a holy and venerable lineage, a Moroccan. My roots, the milieu from which I drew my personal sustenance, as the Moroccans might say (Rosen 1972), were distant, in Europe and America. There, in the space that was "magically" construed for Tuhami and others in his milieu, was the locus of my identity, the ground of my meaningful world, my most significant social horizon, the place where my friends and family dwelt, the center of my ambition, and the privileged arena of my concern. Lhacen's roots, his identity, his meaningful world, his social horizon, his friends and family, his ambition, and his concern, were in Morocco. He was bound in that "chain of consociation" that characterizes Moroccan social life (Rosen 1972a, b and above, p. 77). He was a participant in a society that, as Clifford Geertz argues (somewhat too rhetorically), "does not cope with its diversity by sealing it into castes, isolating it into tribes, dividing it into ethnic groups, or covering it over with some common denominator concept of nationality ... (Geertz 1975, p. 52)." Lhacen could be incorporated into Tuhami's world, could be classified and understood, in a way that I could never be. Lhacen did not possess the privilege of departure that I did. Most Moroccans I met—but, significantly, not Tuhami—were, I suspect, far more envious of my car and my passport than of my other material possessions.

Lhacen's role in the exchanges between Tuhami and me varied over time. At first it was active. It was Lhacen who discovered Tuhami and introduced him to me. Tuhami was for Lhacen a "find" that could help seal his relationship with me (by attesting to his seriousness, his unique capacities, and his understanding of my needs) and affirm my dependency on him. (Lhacen and I often talked, after those first meetings with Tuhami, about Tuhami's potential as an informant.) Lhacen was also able to demonstrate his importance to Tuhami. Not only was he familiar with the ways and language of the *nasrani*—and this familiarity was so important to him that he assumed its importance for others—but he was also able to provide Tuhami with an additional income. I paid Tuhami, as I paid all the Moroccans who took time from their own work to help me. This was expected, and they never bickered or argued or vied with one another for my favor; certainly, Tuhami did not. Payment gave some of them an "understanding" of my demands. They had a job. Tuhami refused this "understanding." He never spoke directly about the money I gave him except when he lost a portion of it and told me he was saving it for his first *jallaba* (see below). Usually, and despite its evident importance for him, he accepted the money with seeming indifference.

In those first meetings, Lhacen mediated my relationship with Tuhami. I was still new to Morocco. I was caught in the whirl of the unfamiliar. I was without anchor and did not have the confidence that comes with knowing the rules of social comportment and cultural evaluation. I was determined not to succumb to the easy aloofness of the total stranger. I felt awkward, confused, lonely even in the presence of my wife, and occasionally afraid. I was terrified of failure and of everything that failure symbolized for me, and I gave expression to this terror, most notably in terms of a loss of *rapport* with the best of my informants. Tuhami was among them, and the sway of my terror and its idiosyncratic expression are evident in my *entretiens* with him. I clung, in those first encounters with Tuhami, not only to a rigid and rather banal conception of my task but to Lhacen as well. He gave me distance and protected me from direct and immediate contact and from the fears and pleasures of such contact. Lhacen was less of a stranger than Tuhami. I imagine that Lhacen served a similar role for Tuhami. He did not, at any rate, get in the way.

Lhacen, and other assistants in Morocco and elsewhere, also gave me access to the more immediate and, as I have said, more intimate world of my informants and friends. It was not *they* who had to give me access. Through Lhacen I had already had my "introduction" to Morocco. They did not have to feed me those representations of culture and society, those clichés, by which the members of any group present themselves to, and defend themselves against, the stranger. (These representations frequently become the stuff of superficial ethnographic description and bolster the stranger's stereotypic view of an alien people.) Rather, Lhacen's presence, and his and therefore my putative savvy, permitted a more direct entrée into the lived world of the Moroccans with whom we worked. Their reflections were not determined by the presence of a "total stranger."* My informants were deprived to some extent of a protective shield, or, perhaps more accurately, they were given, through Lhacen, a new shield. The defenses they did have had to be respected or else overcome through time and warmth and concern.

I am pointing here to certain structural factors in the use of an assistant that may facilitate certain types of research. (Among others would be the slowed rhythm of the meetings, the possibility of observing often illuminating distortions within the translations, the ability to deflect responsibility for questions and misunderstandings to a Third, and the opportunity to discuss the meetings afterwards—an opportunity with obvious implications for the meetings themselves.) Certainly, my relationship with Lhacen and Tuhami was unique. As I remarked earlier, Lhacen had an almost uncanny ability to efface himself in our encounters—an effacing that, paradoxically, did not preclude his active participation as an interpreter and, later as an interpreter-observer in these encounters.† (Self-effacement does

---

*The reflective attitude is always alienating. It demands an interlocutor, a stranger of sorts, who questions the taken-for-granted. The "endopsychic" stranger is of course constrained by the same idiom that articulates the unreflected world. The "real" stranger, inevitably understood through that idiom, is nevertheless occasionally able, through insistence, perspectival difference, projection, and misunderstanding, to break through the idiomatic constraints that fashion the taken-for-granted world and the (conventional) reflections upon it.

†I am fully aware of the alienating quality of this effacement both in terms of the inner dynamics of the triad, Tuhami, Lhacen, and me, and in terms of the work I set Lhacen. It is a given in the triadic relationship and has its implications for all three members, both alone and in various alliances. Lhacen as a *tertius gaudens,* to use Simmel's (1964b) expression, was not, however, without benefit from the arrangement.

not necessarily or even usually come with silence and feigned invisibility. It requires, I believe, the quality that Heidegger [1971] finds characteristic of "equipment" [*das Zeug*] in his famous analysis of Van Gogh's paintings of peasant shoes: *Verläß-lichkeit*, reliability. In the picture, one's attention is called to the shoes and all they evoke; in fact, the peasant "simply wears them." This reliability "first gives to the simple world its security and assures to the earth the freedom of its steady thrust.") We were both strangers and, as such, encouraged openness. The stranger, Simmel (1964a) noted, "often receives the most surprising openness—confidences which sometimes have the character of a confessional and which would be carefully withheld from a more closely related person." However this may be, a certain warmth and sympathy, an approachability, is requisite for such openness even among strangers. Lhacen possessed this, and I believe that I did, at least when I was not frozen in myself. Both of us remarked on the innumerable confidences we had received, over the years, from total strangers.

With time, Lhacen's role in the meetings changed. Tuhami and I recognized our importance for each other.* It was *we* who were meeting. We nevertheless needed Lhacen. We could not go on without him, but in our diverse ways we bracketed him off (never completely, however, for his presence was necessary to our relationship). He was, for Tuhami and me, the Third, who rendered us, in Sartre's (1964) words, an us-object.

> Thus what I experience is a being-outside in which I am organized with the Other in an indissoluble, objective whole, a whole in which I am fundamentally *no longer distinct* from the Other but which I agree in solidarity with the Other to constitute. [Sartre 1964 p. 418]

The essentially conflictual nature of the dual relationship, in Sartre's understanding and in Hegel's and Simmel's too, is, at

---

*Strictly speaking, all my statements here about Tuhami's (or, for that matter, Lhacen's) subjective experience, either in itself or as a component of a we-relationship, must be understood hypothetically, however compelling my basis for inference. The experience of the we-subject, Sartre (1956) notes, "in no way implies a similar and correlative experience in others." The experience of the "we" remains a simple symbol of the longed-for unity of transcendence—a kind of psychological mask for the original conflicts of transcendence, at least in Sartre's Hegelian vision of the relations between consciousnesses.

least for the moment, arrested. Through the Third, embodied here in Lhacen, Tuhami's and my possibilities become "dead possibilities": "But as soon as the Third appears, the Other's possibilities and my own are levelled into dead possibilities, and hence the relationship becomes reciprocal" (Sartre 1964, p. 418).

There is, as Sartre brilliantly portrays in *No Exit* (1945), a fundamental instability in any triadic relationship. There is a constant shifting of alliances and objectifying gazes. These, of course, were all at play in the meetings between Tuhami, Lhacen, and me; but after the first meetings, where Lhacen played an active role, they tended to be subsumed under an intentionally validated, an ad hoc conventional, frame that we had negotiated and now accepted. The meetings were between Tuhami and me. Lhacen was a kind of spokesman for one and then the other of us; that is, he was identified seriatim with each of us as we addressed the other.

It is precisely the conventionally validated frames, ignored by Sartre in *Being and Nothingness* and *No Exit*, that permit a certain (symbolic) constancy in our triadic relations. Within the *established* frame, Lhacen was able to mediate those minor conflicts, those "insignificant differences of opinion, the allusions to an antagonism of personalities, the emergence of quite momentary contrasts of interest and feeling," that continually color, as Simmel (1964b) notes, even the least significant conversations and that certainly colored my conversations with Tuhami.

> Such mediations do not even have to be performed by means of words. A gesture, a way of listening, the mood that radiates from a particular person, are enough to change the difference between two individuals so that they can seek understanding, are enough to make them feel their essential commonness which is concealed under their acutely differing opinions, and to bring this divergence into the shape in which it can be ironed out the most easily. [Simmel 1964b, p. 149]

It is the difference between the frame and the action within the frame that permitted me to assert, and permits me to reassert, the contradictory observation with which I began this discussion of Lhacen's role in my encounter with Tuhami. "Had he not been there, our relationship would have been awkward. Present, he could be ignored and was ignored."

The complicity to bracket off Lhacen—a complicity that the three of us entered into from our different standpoints—not only permitted the conventional framing of our encounter and the maneuvers that occurred within it; it also enabled us to invest Lhacen with symbolic significance. He came to represent the constancy of the frame. Indeed, he became for me, and for Tuhami too, I believe, a symbol of constancy and continuity in a discourse that was threatened with interruption through both fantasied departures (Tuhami's announced intention to make a trip) and my inevitable departure. The fact of departure, which has been largely ignored in the anthropological discussions of field work, plays a determining role in all field research.* The anthropologist as stranger—the wanderer who comes and leaves—is not the stranger of whom Simmel (1964a) writes. His stranger comes to stay. The inevitability of my departure, understood at the outset and ignored thereafter, was reflected not only in the rhythm of my *entretiens* with Tuhami and Lhacen's role in them but also in the recurrent themes of separation, death, castration, and abandonment that punctuated these interviews.†

Lhacen himself played out his symbolic role in mediating conflict. He thus freed Tuhami and me of the burden of constancy and continuity and the fear of death and departure and allowed us the indulgence of symbolic attribution, of transference and countertransference. As controller of the word (and he struggled hard with our words and resented, I thought, my increasing knowledge of Arabic), he came to embody, quite literally, the transcendental Other, that "seat of the Word and guarantor of Truth," which, if I understand Lacan (1966) correctly, is necessary to intersubjective communication (Crapanzano 1978). (Lacan, *pace* Lacan, can be read as a gloss not only on Freud but on Sartre as well.) Lhacen occupied, to speak figuratively, the

---

*See Parin et al. (1971) for examples of the importance of departure in their psychoanalytic interviews with the Anyi.

†Did my "therapeutic" interest in Tuhami's marriage reflect my own anxiety over departure—over abandoning Tuhami? Was I seeking to get myself off the hook by providing him with the possibility of a substitute for me?

place of God—in Sartre's terms, the place of the unrealized Third—within the little universe we three created.*

I exaggerate of course—to point out an irony. We assume that Lhacen played a noteworthy role—a role that governed the exchange between Tuhami and me. He did. Of this there can be no question. Yet I must recognize here a certain "empirical" bias. Possessed of body, Lhacen could embody for me, and perhaps for my readers, highly abstract symbolic meanings. Are Tuhami's demons—who are bodiless, at least as I understand "body"—thus incapable of such "embodiments"? Is it not possible that 'A'isha Qandisha, and the other *jnun* that haunted Tuhami's life, represented the Third, the transcendental locus of meaning, the constancy and continuity of our relationship, of any relationship he had? (I have argued elsewhere [1977a] that possessing spirits provide the possessed with a frozen identity by arresting the dialectics of identity formation.) Or perhaps these spirits render the relationship considerably more complex than I have described it here. I remember working with other Moroccans who, for whatever reasons, suddenly became aware of (we might say, "were spooked by") a demonic presence. My interviews then came to a dead halt. I am not proposing here a mysticism or a philosophy of excessive idealism. I am simply calling attention to a possibility of Otherness that I do not even claim to be Tuhami's. It must be entertained though.

There is, at least for me, an elegiac quality in my re-creation of Tuhami. I recognize, as I write now, the contingency of our existence. How did it come to pass that I, an American anthropologist, should have met Tuhami, a Moroccan tilemaker,

---

*I do not wish to suggest here that Lhacen became the "father" for Tuhami and me. Rather, Lhacen represented one of the functions of the "father": the controller of the word. He was not, however, the source of the word. The resolution of oedipal conflicts can be understood in terms of negotiating and stabilizing the triadic relationship between father, mother, and son. Father and son compete, so to speak, for the word; and, in the classical resolution of the conflict, the father wins out, and the son (and mother) surrenders to him as both source and controller of the word. In the triad formed by Lhacen, Tuhami, and me the functions are split. Lhacen represents the more abstract function of control. I am the initiator of the word that Tuhami gives. In the text I produce here, through my re-presentation of what transpired, I assume all three functions.

and entered so deeply into his life and allowed him to enter so deeply into my own? I write of him now with the hope that something of what I learned from him will serve to correct our own mechanistic presumptions about the nature of man and his relations to his fellow beings. I have placed my personal encounter within an abstract theoretical edifice—a consequence of my encounter—that is neither fully consistent nor as illuminating as I should have liked it to be in order to call attention to these presumptions. With the same end in mind I have played with style and form, and I am satisfied with neither. I have forced myself into the theoretical position that we can know the experience of another only by what he says (as though a text can be understood without the assumption of intersubjectivity), and, at the same time, I have made a plea for a more immediate intersubjective understanding, which I take to be necessary in any social encounter. This paradox, masked in most ordinary, conventional encounters, is brought to light in the ethnographic encounter and may well be its hallmark. "It probably requires cultural insiders," James Clifford (1978) speculates, "to recognize adequately the subtle ruses of individuality where outsiders see only typical behavior." I do not know. Our individuality, Simmel (1965, p. 344) noted, in the same essay I have been quoting, "is supplemented by the Other's view of us, which results in something that we never are purely and wholly." The same must be said for the Other, for Tuhami, in his subjectivity. We should respect in the Other the same mystery we expect others to respect in ourselves. This too is a social fact.

Part Five

I saw Tuhami two days later. I was anxious. I felt the burden of departure. I asked him, evasively, some general questions and then, with a certain relief, more personal ones. I had to assume my new role. I learned that Tuhami usually slept ten hours a night, never took a siesta, and often felt tired. Like most Moroccans I talked to, he had never heard of sleepwalking.

— Have you ever felt as though you were falling?

— Sometimes when I work. Sometimes my mind ['aqel] thinks of something. I don't move. My head spins. Then I need to lean against a wall. If there is no wall, then I fall.

— When did this first happen?

— When I started to work for my boss. He told me to buy some grain for the chickens. I went to pick up the sack. My head began to spin the moment I touched the sack. I fell down and slept all day.

— And then?

— As soon as I touched the sack, my knees went cold. They burned incense for me, but it didn't help.

— Do you remember this?

— No. I remember nothing. Other people told me.

— Did you have a dream then?

— I dreamed there was a woman next to me who didn't say anything.

— Who was she?

— The owner of the place [mula el-blasa].

— Was she pretty?

— She was pretty and had beautiful clothes. She had gold rings. She put her hand on my knee, and, without saying a word, she looked at me. She stayed that way until I woke up. Then she said good-bye.

— How did you feel when you woke up?

155

— Fine.

— You were not sick?

— No.

— How were you feeling before you fell?

— I wasn't thinking of anything in particular. I just fell when I touched the sack.

— What made you fall?

— It is possible the woman caused it. She touched my knees. Ever since then my boss doesn't send me to fetch anything.

— Were you angry at your boss?

— No. I was happy to get the grain. My boss and I fight once a year only. He tells me to do something, and I don't do it. Then we fight. . . .

— Have you ever been dizzy?

— Yes. Time and misery make people dizzy.

— What in the body causes dizziness?

— The heart. You see someone who is married and has children and you have none.

Tuhami considered the heart to be the seat of emotion and (spiritual) desire. He referred to the heart as the king of the body and explained that "anger, love, and sadness all come from it."

— Are you ever sad?

— Yes, but not for long. I go to the movies, and when I leave, I miss what I have seen. I feel sad. I see men who are married and have children. They come to the movies with girls; they have new clothes. I am jealous.

— What do you do when you are sad?

— I curse the world from its beginning to its end. God does not give all men an equal share. To some He gives much. To others He gives little.

— Why?

— It is His will.

I brought up the incident of the drowning and Tuhami's assertion that he has been in misery ever since.

— I have been miserable since then. I have no wife . I've never been married. Every time I want to marry, I can't. If I ask a virgin, she'll say she wants someone educated. If I ask an older woman, she'll say she wants a civil servant. They all say I have a bald head, but they don't know what's in my head. I have always been in misery, and I will always be in misery. If I ever have money, then I'll do what I want. I'll have a wedding, and I'll invite all the mothers of all the daughters who have refused me. I'll see them all the time.

— Why?

— Because we are friends. (*Tuhami was unable to maintain his vindictiveness.*)

Each time I visit these women, they ask me if I want their daughters. I never know if they are serious or if they are teasing me. There is one woman who wants to free me and then give me her daughter. I see the girl in front of my eyes. I will marry her if she is free. I always get the queen when I play cards.

The girl's brother is a secretary in the factory across the road. Yesterday he came over to play cards. My boss asked him if his sister was married. He answered that his mother was considering her marriage and that it depended on me. Her brother had worked in Casablanca and is well educated. He told me he'd try to arrange something. God willing, he will. (*Tuhami was talking on the "plane of reality," but, in all probability, irrealistically. He could not sustain the dissonance.*) I was asleep. I saw that she was going to marry someone else.

— What is her name?

— Fatima. I dreamed that she, Fatima, was in the kitchen cooking. The man she wanted to marry was next to her. I told her, in the dream, that she wouldn't marry him. The next morning I went to see her. He mother made coffee. Fatima asked if I had dreamed of her. I told her I had. She laughed. "I saw you with so-and-so," I said, "but that man will never marry you. He wants to marry another girl who doesn't live far from here." She asked me what she could do about it. I told her that his *métier* is different from hers and that they wouldn't get along.

Within the recitation Tuhami used his dream to manipulate the girl and her mother. Since dreams are believed to be true— and indicative of the future—Tuhami himself was not responsible for the manipulation. Dreams are produced by the soul that wanders from the body and witnesses things elsewhere (Crapanzano 1975).

Tuhami stayed with Fatima and her mother until after supper and then asked the mother if she wanted to go to Moulay Idriss's sanctuary with him. (At first it was not clear whether he had asked the mother or the daughter to accompany him.) Tuhami and Fatima's mother went to the sanctuary. A holy fool there told the mother that her daughter would marry a man whom they did not yet know. "That man knows," the fool said, pointing to Tuhami. Fatima's mother was "crazy with desire" to tell her daughter what the holy fool had said.

— Two days later Fatima and her mother came to the river, near where I work, to wash wool. I saw them and talked to them. I saw that Fatima was sad. Her brother—not the one I know—came over and asked me why I was talking to them.

Fatima's brother assumed, quite naturally, that Tuhami was bothering his mother and sister. Women are not supposed to talk to strange men. A brother is particularly responsible for his sister's virginity. Among the Bedouins of Arabia, it is the brother who must kill the man who has taken advantage of his sister (Musil, 1928).

Fatima's mother explained that Tuhami was a friend. Fatima's brother began to cry. He had known Tuhami's brother 'Ali.

— The moment Fatima saw her brother crying, she fell in love with me. A few days later her mother asked if I would marry her. I said I would have to think about it.

(*I was not sure whether Tuhami was fantasizing or not. He seemed genuinely concerned.*)

— How long ago did she ask you?

— About a month ago.

— Do you want to marry her?

— It is written. I have neither the bride-price nor the time for marriage. There is no money—and it is for that that I cry. It is about that that I think all day and all night. I don't want a modern wedding but an old-fashioned one. It takes seven days.

Tuhami's insistence on his poverty was an excuse, I felt. Moroccan men much poorer than he was manage to marry. The bride-price, however, is usually paid by a father for a son. This payment symbolizes—or so it seemed to me in Tuhami's case—the passing of manhood to the son. The father provides

the son with the means to marry—to have a woman and children. Tuhami had no father and therefore no means, no manhood.

— Why do you want an old-fashioned wedding? (*Tuhami be-
came very evasive. He claimed that it cost less money—a patent untruth.*)
Is this the first time you have wanted to marry?
— Yes.

Tuhami began to cry. In my notes I wrote "like an old
woman," but I don't know why. I could not look at him. I was
overcome with anxious sympathy and concern—and a feeling of
helplessness. I had no faith in my power to help Tuhami.
"Today women all want a gold ring," he said. "But my bones
don't like gold rings." Pinching bones are a symptom of demonic
attack. Tuhami's grandfather, as he was dying, told Mme Jolan
that Tuhami was sick in the bones.* The woman who caused his
knees to go cold was wearing a ring.
Next came one of the first questions Tuhami had ever asked
me.

— What can I do?
— You can marry without a ring.
— The girl even wants me to wear a ring so that everyone will
know I'm married. My boss's daughter has offered to prepare
the wedding feast as a gift.
— Perhaps, this time, it is written.
— I'll try. But first I must go to the shrine of Sidi Sliman Mul
l-Kifan. I'll spend the night there. . . . Perhaps I'll be liberated if I
go to Sidi Sliman's. . . . I don't have any luck. I've tried to buy
things and sell them. I bought five kilos of chick-peas once. It
took me three days to sell them. And all I made was 250 francs.
A friend of mine sold five kilos in one day and made 2,000
francs.
— But it is necessary to try.
— Yes. I try, but nothing ever happens. Someone told me to
go to a seer [*tella'*]. I know what the seer will say. If I do it, I'll fall
sick or die. (*I do not know whether Tuhami meant that he would fall
sick or die if he went to a seer or if he married.*)
— What will the seer say?

*See above, footnote, p. 55.

— I know what she'll say. (*It was not clear to me who the "she" was—the seer or someone else.*) My sister went to a seer [*shuwwafa*] for me. The seer told my sister that I should visit Sidi Sliman. Then, she said, I'll have luck and marry. She asked my sister to tell her when I marry. She said she'll explain everything then. She said that my teeth have fallen out and that I will replace them and that I will have children.

Tuhami was trying to talk himself into confidence. Again it was the saints who would give him his strength.

"You will have a dream tonight," I said finally. I had no idea if I was doing the right thing, but I had to do something. The idiom seemed strange and yet, uncannily, familiar. "You will have a dream tonight. It will be very frightening because you will recognize someone. Once you recognize that person, you will be liberated." I repeated my instructions twice—firmly.

— I want to marry. I want to marry. I will fight hard. They will try to present me with another, but I will refuse. (*Tuhami was very excited.*)
— You will be as strong as they are. (*I assumed that the "they" were the* jnun. *Tuhami smiled.*)

I offered to drive him to the village where Sidi Sliman's sanctuary is located. He said he wanted to go with a neighbor. I agreed to take the neighbor too. As I said good-bye to him, Tuhami said mysteriously, "Sidi Sliman does not like the Gnawa. Rocks always fall on them." The Gnawa are black trance-dancers who know the favorite rhythms of many of the female *jnun*. 'A'isha Qandisha is often called 'A'isha Gnawiyya. I did not know what to make of Tuhami's observation.

·   ·   ·

The following morning I drove Tuhami to Sidi Sliman's sanctuary. It is located on the side of a cliff overlooking a river. Tuhami's neighbor could not come; it was he, I learned, who had sold the chick-peas for a profit. Tuhami had dreamed that he was at Sidi Sliman's.

— My boss's wife and daughter were there joking. I asked why they were joking. They asked me why I hadn't come to them. I said I would come in the morning. Then my boss repeated again and again: "Come, come, come." I woke up.

Tuhami thought that the dream encouraged him to visit Sidi Sliman's shrine. I said nothing. The saintly and the practical (his boss's daughter's offer to prepare the wedding feast) were conjoined. Tuhami also told me that he had lost the money I had given him yesterday. He dreamed that a woman had taken it from him. We arrived at the sanctuary before I could ask him who the woman was. I left him to spend the night. Two days later I saw him again.

— How was your visit?

— I came back yesterday morning. I walked all the way back. (*Tuhami was always proud of his walking.*) I went to sleep there. I saw Hassan. He told me what I wanted I could have. But I would have to wait a while. "If you want to buy and sell things, you must wait until the end of Ramadan. If you must sell things before then, sell them in small quantities." That is what he said.

— Who is Hassan?

— He is a friend, a policeman. I've been to his house. . . . Hassan asked me how long it had been since I visited Sidi Sliman. I told him it had been a long time. I asked him how long he had been at the sanctuary. "Thirteen years," he answered. I said that is like yesterday. He told me to come in the summer. I promised to come for seven days.

— Have you known Hassan for a long time?

— I met him at the movies. He's always there. When he saw me, he told me I would succeed. I told him it must be soon, for my heart is heavy with worry.

Tuhami seemed evasive. I knew that he had money worries; he was paid by the tile, and during the rainy season—it was just beginning—he could not work. The tiles had to be sun-dried before they were put in the kiln. I could not help thinking that Tuhami suspected that my departure would be soon. I had told him at our first meeting that I would probably leave Meknes before winter. It was the middle of November. I had decided to put off talking to him about it until I could in some way prepare him. I spent the rest of the interview trying to form a chronology of the principal events in his life. Now that he had told me about the drowning, he seemed better able to organize his personal history—to talk on what I took to be the plane of reality. (I have used this information in the earlier sections of his portrait.) I continued the chronology on the following day. Tuhami's descriptions were very straightforward; he was in a good mood. I was surprised that he did not mention his marriage problems, but I did not think that I should bring them up myself. What could I do, really? I was leaving in three days. I had arranged to see Tuhami two more times. Afterwards, he and several other friends were coming to our house for a farewell dinner.

•   •   •

In our next-to-last interview, Tuhami told me about a friend who had given him an amulet.

— He fell sick because he didn't get along with the demons [*l-ariah*] that are in me. (*Tuhami stated this matter-of-factly.*)

— Are there several demons in you?

— There are a lot. Yesterday I tried to fight them all night, especially the women. There were sixty women. Some had children. Some were pregnant. Some were giving birth. Some had no children. She who bothers me, she was not among them. She prevents me from marrying. Each woman wanted to sit next to me. I said I couldn't stand this. "What do you want?" I asked. "If you want me to burn spices, I'll burn them." They said: "We want nothing—only that you remain the way you are." They asked me why I talked to other women and not to them. I'll burn spices in my room. That will keep them away. I'll see which one will remain. The last to leave will be the one behind me—who didn't want the Koranic writings.

I did not push Tuhami. He seemed satisfied with his solution. I decided to ask him what he had done all day yesterday—to emphasize the practical, the "real."

— I woke for prayers at dawn and then had breakfast. I sat thinking until you arrived. I was thinking about my life, about whether I will succeed or fail. I don't know. If I don't have luck this year, then I will never have luck.

— And what happened after you saw us?

— I went to buy vegetables. I talked to the greengrocer whom

I know. He asked where I had been. I told him I was always around. He asked me when I was going to have a celebration.

— What did he mean?

— A wedding. I answered, "God willing, this year." "That's it," the greengrocer said. "You must have one." I went back to my room. My boss was there. He asked where I had been. I told him I had been on an errand. He told me to get some cards. We played cards, and then I went to the tailor to get my *jallaba*. [Tuhami had saved the money I had given him over the last few months to buy a *jallaba*, his first.]

That was the end of my day. I went into my room. I prepared my dinner: meat, vegetables, and bread. I sat in my room alone, except for God. God was with me. I did nothing. I said my prayers and made tea. I drank the tea and thought of God until I fell asleep. I slept until early morning prayers.'

— When did the women surround you?

— Just before I got up. [A sleeper is considered to be particularly vulnerable to demonic influence just before waking. Hypnopomic images are attributed to Shitan.]

— Did you talk to anyone else yesterday?

— No.

— Are there many demons (*l-ariah*) in you?

— Half remain in my house. Half come with me, always. The woman who is attached to me is always in my house.

— What would happen if you left your house forever?

— If I move, she'll move. Even if I tried to move, I'd have to come back to my house. The others say I have to live there. I must come back even if I moved as far as Moulay 'Ali Zahara's. . . . (*Tuhami listed several more saints.*) They are all in my room. There is one who never leaves my room. His name is Lahadi ben el-Mlah. He lives in my room.

[The confusion of saint and *jinn* is not unusual. Westermarck (1926) reported examples of this sort in 1926, and I frequently observed it in my work with other Moroccans.]

— What is he like?

— Sometimes he is nice; sometimes he is mean.

— Does he enter your body?

— No. He is always in my room, in the corner. He sits next to me. He keeps saying, "You will have nothing until I let you go." If I ever get something, it will not be until the 'Ayed s-Seghrir.

[It was not to have been until the *musem* in the village of Moulay Idriss. Now that the *musem* had taken place, it was not to be until the 'Ayed s-Seghrir, the feast that closes Ramadan, three months off.]

It is possible that a woman will tell me to make a trip. I'll take a long trip. I'll make it in a car. I don't know where. That is how I spend my day. I don't move. (*Tuhami sat still and silent, with a sad face.*)

— Do you and Lahadi have conversations?

— Yes.

— What do you talk about?

— "Why are you angry? What are you thinking? Why did you throw plates around?" he asks me. "It all comes from God," he says. "Be patient." I ask him why I am alone. "There are a lot of workers here. They could have taken my place for a while," I say. "They have all left and bought houses and cars and are married. I'm always stuck here." Lahadi tells me that I can do nothing, that it is God who wills it. I answer "There are workers here who go with girls and have a good time. And I? I stay here thinking all the time." "God," Lahadi says, "does not want you to frequent women—especially during the three months before the end of Ramadan. You must go to the movies. You must walk to the market. You must look around. In the evening you must come home and pray. You must ask God to free you." I say I will.

— When did Lahadi first visit you?

— He is always with me. The others are always with me too—in me. Except when I was at Sidi Sliman's.

— You were strong that day.

— Because I was prepared to have a big battle with them. I went there and told them that I had come to lodge a complaint against a woman who has followed me for twenty years. I have not been able to escape her. God willing, I'll visit Sidi Sliman's at the 'Ayed s-Seghrir and spend three days there. It is certain that I'll cut relations with them then.

— When did the woman begin to follow you?

— She was dressed as a woman. She ate with me and slept with me. Then she didn't want to leave. I wanted her to, but she wanted to marry me. I refused. I must also have a *real* woman—two wives. I must shave and dress well.

— When did the woman follow you for the first time?

— In the room I live in now.

— Did you still work for Mme Jolan?

— She was already with me. (*There was excitement in Tuhami's voice.*) I didn't know she was an invisible.

— When did you know?

— Seven years ago. I knew by her feet. Her feet were not like ours. They were camel's feet.

— You hadn't seen her feet until then?

— No.

— When did she visit you?

— I thought she was human.

— When did she visit you for the first time?

— I was working for Mme Jolan. My grandfather was dead. I worked for Mme Jolan. I slept in the room where I sleep now. One night I left work and was going home, and on the road I met the woman. She greeted me. She asked if she could spend the night with me. I asked if she were alone. "I'm not from around here," she said. "I'm from a place a little way off." I told her to come on in with me. She came in and said she liked my room. I said that it was a poor man's room but had everything. "It's the life of a bachelor," she said. I agreed. "A bachelor sleeps all around." "You'll marry soon," she answered. I prepared *tajin*. We ate and drank tea. My heart was not afraid. I looked at her. She was really a woman. When it was time to go to sleep, I said, "You are my guest. Sleep on the bed. I'll sleep on the floor." She answered that she wanted to sleep with me. I said that it was better if we slept apart. "You don't want to admit that you want to sleep with me," the woman said, "but you do!" I slept next to her and made love to her. Then the woman said that she liked to be with me and that she saw me always. "You see me always?" I asked. "How is that? I never see you." "I'm always passing you. I always see you, and you see me too," she answered. "I don't know," I said. Then she said good-bye. I wanted to give her a little money, but she refused it. We said we would see each other again. She was away for a month.

One day she came, and I suspected something wasn't right. I didn't want to talk to her. She began to fondle me and kiss me. "I want to know who you are," I demanded. "I'm a woman like all women," she answered. "Ask others who know me. They'll tell you." I told her that it was all right but that I didn't want to make love to her. "Why?" she asked. I said, "Next time."

She didn't come again for two years. Then she came back. She

was very flirtatious and had on new clothes. I was near Mme
Jolan's factory. She was walking in front of the factory. She
signaled me, "Tonight." I agreed. I bought milk to prepare coffee. She came over shortly after I finished work and sat down. I
was blowing the fire with the bellows when she came in. She had
on her slippers. [Moroccans remove their shoes and slippers upon
entering a house.] I looked at her feet. She kept looking at me. She
suspected I saw something. "Why are you looking at my feet?"
she asked. "You have pretty thighs. That's why," I answered.
Then she said: "Now you know me. I won't hide." she took off
her slippers, her scarf, her *jallaba*. "Why didn't you tell me this
the first time?" I asked. "You've tricked me. Now that I know,
I'm finished. I don't want to talk to you again." "If you want to
marry," she said, "I'll choose the woman. She'll be my choice. It
is I who command now. If you don't accept, you'll remain a
bachelor for the rest of your life." That is where we left it. She
never came back.

Tuhami was absolutely calm as he told me this story. I did not
know what to believe. He was expressing himself so much more
realistically than he ever had before.

— How did you feel when you saw the woman's feet?
— My head changed. My head was swollen. My mind ['aqel]
told me to put a knife in the woman. But I had no steel knife. If I
had had a steel knife, I would have killed her. I would have
plunged the knife in the earth, and then it would have been I
who commanded. She would have had to agree with me always.
She would remain there as though in a bottle. I could have done
anything. I could have slapped her. I could have beat her. She
would have had to run errands for me. Since then . . . . (*Tuhami's
excitement drained away. But the emotion that had been missing in his
initial recitation was still there.*) Since then my affairs have not been
very good. If she came now—now that I am well trained—I
would win.
— She is afraid. (*My words were midway between a question and a
suggestion.*)
— It is too late. Now she commands.
— How can you escape?
— I'll see. Perhaps the saint we visited (*Sidi Sliman, I supposed*)

will help. There are also spices. They'll help me. A woman who was never able to marry tried them and got married. "She" came to her that night and gave her a good blow on the thigh. The woman is my neighbor.

— What was happening in your life when you first saw her?

Tuhami said nothing. On a hunch (at the time, I was somewhat simplistically convinced that the "she" was a demonic mask for Mme Jolan and her sister) I asked:

— Was Sylvie there?

— No. Sylvie was not there. (*Tuhami did not seem the least surprised by my question.*) Sylvie came after I already knew her. Sylvie came. Her children were sick. She told the workers to say a prayer for her children. She promised that if the children got better she would give a celebration. She did. I was working for Mme Jolan and earned my twenty-five francs a day. Afterward, I ran errands for Sylvie, and she gave me fifty francs.

— But what was happening when you first saw her?

— Nothing. My body was fine.

— Do you remember what you were doing that day?

— I worked all day.

— What was happening in Mme Jolan's life?

— She was watching the poultry. We were giving the chickens grain. When the woman came the first time, she saw me there. She came back later and asked Mme Jolan where I was. Mme Jolan called me and told me that a woman was looking for me.

— Was she there with Mme Jolan?

— She was there with Mme Jolan, on the roof.

— Whom did she look like?

— She looked just like Khadija bint Fatna. She was a little taller. Otherwise the same.

Khadija was an extremely fat, ugly girl who lived next door to Lhacen. Her mother, Fatna, had often gone to Tuhami to ask for help in getting her married off. She was so ugly that no man had wanted her. Tuhami, however, often joked with her; he gave her magic to pass her exams, but she failed anyway. He told her that that was because she had not gone to Sidi 'Ali's sanctuary as he had instructed her to do.

— Did Mme Jolan ever mention her to you?

— No. Mme Jolan did not talk to me about women. She did not know whether I did things like that or not.

— What happened the next time you saw her?

— I was working in the factory. I thought of her from time to time. It was all the same to me.

— Did you have girls at that time?

— No.

Much to my surprise, Tuhami denied that he had ever had a girl at Casablanca. He now said he first slept with a girl in Moulay Bushta's village.

— There was a big wedding in Meknes. Mme Jolan and her children were invited. I met a girl there who had just been divorced. She came from Moulay Bushta's village. She told me to come and see her the next time I was there. When I went there, I met her. I spent fifteen days with her. I have never slept with another woman. (*I did not doubt Tuhami*).

— Had the other woman already shown her feet?

— No. I didn't know her yet. It was when I left that girl that I knew the other was a *jinn*.

— Since then? (*Tuhami said nothing.*) You are not able to have girls?

— No. This woman, Lalla 'A'isha, does not stay with me. She just comes to sleep with me. She is always about twenty-nine, thirty, or thirty-one years old. She never goes to the movies. If I talk to a girl about sex, I'm sure she'll go to the police. She has done this so that I will not talk to other women. There are girls who want to sleep with me, but I can only signal them to keep away.

(*Tuhami was now talking personally. He had abandoned the neuter pronoun of his recitations—and of my questions.*)

— Have you tried?

— No. I can't even try. I know that she will go to the police. Now I go to the movies. There are girls I know at the movies, but I can't even talk to them.

— Can't you try? Who will listen to the girl?

— The police. It's impossible for me.

— Why don't you go to an older woman, one with experience?

— She won't let me.

(*I tell Tuhami not to be afraid of impotence.*)

I can sleep with any woman. That is not the problem. Even before I sleep with them, I have problems.

(*I tell Tuhami—and Lhacen does too—that we were all afraid before marriage. We were afraid of responsibility. . . . Tuhami smiled.*)

It is not thinking of responsibilities that is the problem. It is "she." I don't know what she wants. But now Sidi Sliman is taking care of that.

— You yourself must be strong like a steel knife.

— I will. I'll buy spices and empty the room. Then I will dream of what will happen to me.

• • •

I prefaced the typed notes of our last interview with the following words, as if I were rationalizing to some unknown interlocutor—to my own Lahadi: "This was the last interview I was to have with Tuhami, and I did not want to leave him dangling. I therefore let him tell me his dreams and interpret them himself. As he seemed quite encouraged, I pushed the positive elements in his interpretation and avoided all other insights."

"I used the spices yesterday," Tuhami began, as soon as we sat down. I was relieved by the ease with which he began to describe his dream and by his positive feelings toward me.

— I was fighting the women all night long. They asked why. Why had I burned the spices? Why had I? I answered: "Because you do not want to leave me." Two women came; they said they were from the Guerwon tribe. This was not true. They came from the town of Moulay Idriss. They put down some clothes near my room and pretended they had come to see a woman. I was at the grocer's, and, on my return, one of the women asked if she could leave the clothes at my place. I said yes. I picked up the clothes. They were very heavy. I thought the sacks were filled with clothes, but they were filled with meal. When I got to my room, I found that my clothes had disappeared. I said: "Well, you've taken my clothes. Who has taken my clothes?" A man in my room cried out: "You must go to Mahdi's in the *mellah* [the old Jewish quarter]." I did not want to listen to him. He grabbed me. I fought back. "Don't touch me," I said. I drew out a knife. I threatened him. "Where did you get the knife?" he asked. I told him I had six knives. "It's incredible," the man said; "I tell you to go to Mahdi's house. What you will see there! It will interest you. If it does, then listen to him. If it doesn't, then forget it." I said, "All right." The man then said, "Take the gifts the women have given you and go to Mahdi."

I was on my way to the *mellah*. There were two women on the road. "You want to see things there," they said. "But it is us. You must not go alone. We will go with you. We will see if she wants to marry." I said, "All right." The women said, "All right." They said "Good-bye." I then saw a group of boys. The boys asked: "Why are you liked by all the women, and we are not?" Someone tried to punch me, but he did not hit me. I threw dust in their eyes. They were cleaning the dust out of their eyes, and I went to my house. When I entered, I saw a woman sitting next to me. "You must not be afraid," she said. "You must not think. You will have what you want. Now there is only one man who remains. You will kill him. Then you will succeed!" We were drinking tea. A few minutes later, someone knocked on my door. I left my room to see who it was. I found a man behind the door. The moment he saw me, he flew off like a bird. When I saw him flying, I spread my hands like wings and cried aloud, "Allah." I began to fly after him, crying "Allah, Allah, Allah." The man flew and landed in a farm. I landed next to him and said, "All right, and now?" The man answered, "I'll bring in my poultry. I'll collect my money and see what I'll do with you." I said, "If I let you do that, you'll go free. I'll kill you first and then. . . . " "No, don't kill me," the man cried out. "Tell me what you want." "I'm looking for someone who is bothering me," I said. The man said it was not him. "I'll look for the person who is bothering you, be it man or woman. I'll do it. Wait an hour?" I agreed. A few minutes later the man came back. "I have found them sleeping," he said. "I don't want to wake them." "Is it a man, a woman, or a virgin?" I asked. "It is 'she,'" the man answered. "A virgin. What do you want to ask her, exactly? I'll give you the answer." I asked: "Is it she who has made me impotent? I want to attack her because she has bothered me a lot."

(Tuhami was very nervous—blushing, too.)

"That's easy," the man said. "No, it is difficult," I answered; "for me it is difficult." The man moved his head from left to right. And I hit him on the neck. He fell to the ground. I took two chickens, a rooster, and two hens from the man's poultry. I put them in my pocket. I flew off. I flew over a cemetery. In the cemetery I saw a woman preparing something. I was very scared. I cried out to a friend. (He is dead now; his name was Qaddur.) "Oh! My friend, Qaddur, help me with my problems," I cried. "I have many problems this year." I knew I was flying like a bird, but one day I would be in a cemetery. That is the way it is with men. I would be there one day. I woke up.

Tuhami paused. I was exhausted. It was a dream-epic, a symbolic biography, a philosophy of resignation—and of hope, too, I had to believe.

— What do you think about it?
— The dream was good, except when I found the meal. When someone receives meal in a dream, he will be depressed. *(The sack of meal is, of course, a frequent theme in Tuhami's recitations.)* I know the house in the *mellah* well. There is a woman there. Her husband went to France. For three years now he has not sent her a letter or a cent.
— What does it all mean?
— I don't know. Where I am to go, there I will be. Perhaps the woman wants to marry me. Her aunt always asks me to marry her. "I'll take care of everything," she says. "Don't bring any man. I don't trust them," she says. Her husband is in France, and I don't know what will happen. He has sent nothing. I don't know whether he is alive or dead. On Thursday I'll visit her. I don't have a choice. Even if she were ninety, I'd marry her. I have no choice. I don't want to remain in my room.

I tell Tuhami that finding the meal—the depression—took place at the beginning of the dream. The depression will be short-lived. The flying means that he will be a man and that he will have the life of a man.

— It is not men who will be depressed. It is the demons of the house [*mwalin dar*] who will be depressed. The woman, too, when I visit her, will be depressed. She is already depressed because her aunt tells her to marry. She keeps waiting for her husband. The aunt says she'll take care of the divorce and everything. I will not be depressed. I have done what is necessary. I have killed the man. I will see what will happen—if it is her or someone else.

I agree with Tuhami. I stress that he himself has a choice. Flying like a bird means liberty, I tell him.

— That is what I told you yesterday. I bothered them, and I have succeeded. When I dream, I dream of things that are true. I dream and fight. I never call to anyone but Allah. Not to my friends. Not to saints. Today I find that my limbs are strong. Tonight I'll do the same. I'll do it until they say yes or no. When you burn spices, it strangles the others at the neck. The woman who sold me the spices—today she is sick. I told her that when I have more freedom, I'll take care of her. I'll bring her penny-royal, and she will get better.

(*Tuhami paused, and then, almost as an afterthought, he continued.*)

I know it will work. I'll have my freedom because I saw Mme Jolan in my room. The moment I woke up, I saw her.

— Did she say anything?

— She said: "May God help you." She left, but it wasn't really her. It was "she"—'A'isha. Today I feel like a bird. Last night was a miracle.

And so it was Tuhami who gave me the courage to say what I had to say. I told him that we were leaving. At first he did not understand. Then he did; he showed no strong emotion. He accepted my departure with resignation, just as he accepted the innumerable disappointments in his life. At dinner that night— and unlike most of my other friends who came—Tuhami maintained a strong sense of himself, of his independence and his dignity. He kept the conversation gay when the others would have turned it maudlin and sentimental. When I drove him home, I gave him a large steel hunting knife. I told him that I hoped the knife would give him strength and be the key to his liberation. He was at a loss for words and put the gift quickly away. Lhacen kissed him goodbye. He was surprised when I kissed him goodbye too, and he mumbled something about my coming back to Meknes soon. His last words were a promise that he would be strong. Lhacen and I watched him make his way down the narrow path that led to his house. We were both crying.

Epilogue

Lhacen visited Meknes six weeks after I had left the city. Tuhami told him that on the night of our farewell dinner he had been attacked by ten thousand women who danced around him like wasps and that he had overcome them, thanks to the knife I had given him. He said he was waiting until the 'Ayed s-Seghrir to visit Sidi Sliman Mul l-Kifan's sanctuary. Then he would know what was written for him. Lhacen did not have the heart to ask him the name of the boy who had drowned. We both thought it might have been Qaddur.

For about a year I received occasional letters from Tuhami, and then they stopped. They had been written by paid scribes and were little more than ornate greetings—expressions of best wishes and good health and the hope that, God willing, my wife and I would be coming back soon.

In 1973 I finally arranged to return to Morocco for a visit. Shortly before I left New York, I received a letter from Tuhami's half-brother, whom I did not know. He wrote that, since Tuhami's death, he had kept and cherished a photograph of me, his dear friend; he asked for a work contract. Arriving in Meknes, I went to the factory where Tuhami had worked and learned that Tuhami had been dead for about a year. His boss was away, and the worker who told me about his death had not known him. The worker thought that Tuhami had perhaps had a bad liver. He died on the way to the hospital. I tried to find his stepbrother, but no one at the address he had sent me had ever heard of him. I did not know his sister's address.

Oh, Tuhami, that is the way it is with men.

Bibliography

Abrams, M. H.
1971 *Natural Supernaturalism: Tradition and Revolution in Romantic Literature.* New York: Norton.

Aeschylus
1959 *Eumenides.* Translated by Richmond Lattimore. In David Grene and R. Lattimore, eds., *The Complete Greek Tragedies,* vol. 1. Chicago: University of Chicago Press.

Africanus, Leo
1956 *Description de l'Afrique,* vol. 1. Translated by A. Epaulard. Paris: Maisonneuve.

Berger, Peter L., and Thomas Luckmann
1967 *The Social Construction of Reality: A Treatise in the Sociology of Knowledge.* New York: Anchor Books.

ben Jelloun, Taher
1979 Marrakech: La médina est malade. *Le Monde,* January 28–29, p. 18.

Blanchot, M.
1955 *L'Espace littéraire.* Paris: Gallimard.

Brignon, Jean, et al.
1967 *Histoire du Maroc.* Casablanca: Librairie Nationale.

Brunel, René
1926 *Essai sur la confrérie religieuse des 'Aissaoua au Maroc.* Paris: Paul Geuthner.
1955 *Le Monachisme errant dans l'Islam: Sidi Heddi et les Heddawa.* Publications de l'Institut des Hautes Etudes: Morocains, no. 48. Paris: Larose.

Clifford, James
1978 Hanging Up Looking Glasses at Odd Corners: Ethnobiographical Perspectives. *Harvard English Studies* 8:41–56.

Crapanzano, Vincent
1972   *The Fifth World of Forster Bennett: Portrait of a Navaho.* New York: Viking.
1973   *The Hamadsha: A Study in Moroccan Ethnopsychiatry.* Berkeley: University of California Press.
1975   Saints, *Jnun*, and Dreams: An Essay in Moroccan Ethnopsychology. *Psychiatry* 38:145–59.
1977a   Introduction. Pp. 1–40 in V. Crapanzano and V. Garrison, eds., *Case Studies in Spirit Possession.* New York: John Wiley.
1977b   The Life History in Anthropological Field Work. *Anthropology and Humanism Quarterly* 2:3–7.
1977c   Mohammed and Dawia. Pp. 141–76 in V. Crapanzano and V. Garrison, eds., *Case Studies in Spirit Possession.* New York: John Wiley.
1977d   The Writing of Ethnography. *Dialectical Anthropology* 2:69–73.
1978   Lacan's *Ecrits. Canto* 2:183–91.
1980   *Rite of Return: Circumcision in Morocco.* Vol. 9 of *The Psychoanalytic Study of Society,* edited by Warner Muensterberger and L. Bryce Boyer. New York: Library of Psychological Anthropology.

D'Annunzio, G.
1900   *Trionfo della Morte.* Milan: Fratelli Traves.

Dermenghem, Emile
1954   *Le Culte des saints dans l'Islam maghrébin.* Paris: Gallimard.

Dethier, Jean
1973   Evolution of Concepts of Housing, Urbanism, and Country Planning in a Developing Country: Morocco, 1900–1972. Pp. 197–243 in L. C. Brown, ed., *From Madina to Metropolis: Heritage and Change in the Near Eastern City.* Princeton: Darwin Press.

Devereux, George
1967   *From Anxiety to Method in the Behavioral Sciences.* The Hague and Paris: Mouton.

Dwyer, Daisy Hilse
1978   *Images and Self-Images: Male and Female in Morocco.* New York: Columbia University Press.

Eikelman, Dale F.
1976   *Moroccan Islam: Tradition and Society in a Pilgrimage Center.* Austin: University of Texas Press.

1977   Ideological Change and Regional Cults: Mar-
            aboutism and Ties of "Closeness" in Western
            Morocco. In Richard P. Werbner, ed., *Regional
            Cults*. A.S.A. Monographs, no. 10. New York:
            Academic Press.
1978   The Art of Memory: Islamic Education and Its So-
            cial Reproduction. *Comparative Studies in Society and
            History* 20: 485–516.

Eliade, Mircea
1954   *The Myth of the Eternal Return*. New York: Pan-
            theon.

Erikson, Erik
1969   *Gandhi's Truth: On the Origins of Militant Nonviolence*.
            New York: Norton.

Farès, B.
1961/62   Article "'Ird." *Encyclopaedia of Islam (New Edition)*,
            vol. 4, pp. 77–78.

Fedotov, G. P.
1966   *The Russian Religious Mind*, vol. 1. Cambridge,
            Mass.: Harvard University Press.

Franchi, Jean
1959   Urbanisation d'un Bidonville: Bordj Moulay Omar
            (Meknès). *Bulletin économique et sociale du Maroc*
            23:255–91.

Frye, Northrop
1976   History and Myth in the Bible. Pp. 1–19 in A.
            Fletcher, ed., *The Literature of Fact*. New York: Co-
            lumbia University Press.

Gadamer, Hans-Georg
1960   *Wahrheit und Methode*. Tübingen: J. C. B. Mohr.

Garrison, Vivian
1977   The "Puerto Rican Syndrome" in Psychiatry and
            Espiritismo. Pp. 383–449 in V. Crapanzano and
            V. Garrison, eds., *Case Studies in Spirit Possession*.
            New York: John Wiley.

Geertz, Clifford
1968   *Islam Observed: Religious Development in Morocco and
            Indonesia*. New Haven: Yale University Press.
1975   On the Nature of Anthropological Understanding.
            American Scientist 63:47–53.

Gulick, John
1973   The Ethos of Insecurity. Paper prepared for con-
               ference on Psychology and Near Eastern Studies,
               Princeton University, May 1973.

Hart, David M.
1976   *The Aith Waryaghar of the Moroccan Rif.* Viking Fund
               Publications in Anthropology, no. 55. Tucson:
               University of Arizona Press.

Heidegger, Martin
1971   The Origin of the Work of Art. Translated by
               Albert Hofstadter. Pp. 17–81 in *Poetry, Language,
               and Thought.* New York: Harper & Row.

Hegel, G. W. F.
1966   *The Phenomenology of Mind.* trans. James Baillie.
               London: George Allen & Unwin.

Hymes, Dell
1974   *Reinventing Anthropology.* New York: Vintage.

Jung, C. G.
1961   *Memories, Dreams, and Reflections.* Translated by
               Richard and Clara Winston. New York: Vintage.

Kierkegaard, Søren
1964   *Repetition: An Essay in Experimental Psychology.*
               Translated by Walter Lowrie. New York: Harper
               & Row.

Lacan, Jacques
1966   *Ecrits.* Paris: Seuil.

Langer, Suzanne K.
1957   *Philosophy in a New Key: A Study in the Symbolism of
               Reason, Rite, and Art.* Cambridge, Mass.: Harvard
               University Press.

Langness, L. L., and G. Frank
1978   Fact, Fiction, and the Ethnographic Novel. *An-
               thropology and Humanism Quarterly* 3:18–22.

Leenhardt, Maurice
1979   *Do Kamo.* Translated by Basia M. Gulati. Chicago:
               University of Chicago Press.

LeTourneau, Roger
1949   *Fès avant le Protectorat.* Publications de l'Institut des
               Hautes Etudes Marocaines, no. 45. Casablanca:
               S.M.L.E.

1965   *La Vie quotidienne à Fès en 1900.* Paris: Hachette.

Levy, Reuben
1962   *The Social Structure of Islam.* Cambridge, Eng.: At the University Press.

Lewis, Ioan
1972   *The Anthropologist's Muse.* London: London School of Economics and Political Science.

Mannoni, O.
1956   *Prospero and Caliban: The Psychology of Colonialization.* Translated by Pamela Powesland. New York: Praeger.

Mauss, Marcel
1967   *The Gift: Forms and Functions of Exchange in Archaic Societies.* Translated by Ian Cunnison. New York: Norton.

May, Rollo
1968   The Delphic Oracle as Therapist. Pp. 211–318 in Marianne L. Simmel, ed., *The Reach of the Mind: Essays in Memory of Kurt Goldstein.* New York: Springer.

Mead, George Herbert
1964   *On Social Psychology.* Chicago: University of Chicago Press.

Meakin, B.
1901   *The Land of the Moors.* London: Swan Sonnenschein.

Mercier, H.
1951   *Dictionnaire Arabe-Français.* Rabat: Editions La Porte.

Mernissi, Fatima
1975   *Beyond the Veil: Male-Female Dynamics in a Modern Muslim Society.* New York: Schenkman.

Munn, Nancy
1973   Symbolism in Ritual Context: Aspects of Symbolic Action. In J. J. Honigman, ed., *Handbook of Social and Cultural Anthropology.* Chicago: Rand McNally.

Musil, Alois
1928   *The Manners and Customs of the Rwala Bedouins.* New York: American Geographical Society.

Nash, Dennison
1963   The Ethnologist as Stranger: An Essay in the
            Sociology of Knowledge. *Southwestern Journal of
            Anthropology* 19:149–69.

Nerval Gérard de
1966   *Les Nuits d'Octobre.* Pp. 77–118 in *Oeuvres,* vol. 1.
            Paris: Bibliothèque de la Pléiade.

Nicholson, Reynold A.
1963   *The Mystics of Islam.* London: Routledge & Kegan
            Paul.

Ortigues, Marie-Cecile, and Edmond Ortigues
1906   *Oedipe africain.* Paris: Plon.

Parin, Paul; Fritz Morgenthaler; and Goldy Parin-Matthèy
1971   *Fürchte deinen Nächsten wie dich selbst: Psychoanalyse
            und Gesellschaft am Modell der Agni in Westafrika.*
            Frankfurt am Main: Suhrkamp.

Pickthall, Mohammed Marmaduke
1963   *The Meaning of the Glorious Koran.* New York:
            Mentor.

Rabinow, Paul
1975   *Symbolic Domination: Cultural Form and Historical
            Change in Morocco.* Chicago: University of Chicago
            Press.
1977   *Reflections on Fieldwork in Morocco.* Berkeley: Uni-
            versity of California Press.

Rosaldo, Renato
1976   The Story of Tukbaw. Pp. 121–51 in F. E. Rey-
            nolds and D. Capps, eds. *The Biographical Process:
            Studies in the History and Psychology of Religion.* The
            Hague and Paris: Mouton.

Rosen, Lawrence
1972a   Muslim-Jewish Relations in a Moroccan City. *Inter-
            national Journal of Middle Eastern Studies* 3:435–49.
1972b   The Social and Conceptual Framework of Arab-
            Berber Relations in Central Morocco. Pp. 155–73
            in E. Gellner and C. Micaud, eds., *Arabs and Berbers.*
            Lexington, Mass.: Lexington Books.

Said, Edward
1978   *Orientalism.* New York: Pantheon.

Sartre, Jean-Paul
1945   *Huit clos.* Paris: Gallimard.

1956   *Being and Nothingness: An Essay in Phenomenological Ontology.* Translated by Hazel E. Barnes. New York: Philosophical Library.
1964   *Saint Genet: Actor and Martyr.* Translated by Bernard Frechtman. New York: Mentor.

Schutz, Alfred
1944   The Stranger: An Essay in Social Psychology. *American Journal of Sociology* 49:498–507.
1962   *Collected Papers,* vol. 1. The Hague: Martinus Nijhoff.
1967   *The Phenomenology of the Social World.* Evanston: Northwestern University Press.

Simmel, Georg
1964a   The Stranger. Pp. 402–8 in K. H. Wolff, ed. and trans., *The Sociology of Georg Simmel.* New York: Free Press.
1964b   The Triad. Ibid., pp. 145–69.
1965   How Is Society Possible? Pp. 337–56 in K. H. Wolff, ed. and trans., *Essays on Sociology, Philosophy, and Aesthetics.* New York: Harper & Row.

Turner, Victor
1974   *Dramas, Fields, and Metaphors: Symbolic Action in Human Society.* Ithaca: Cornell University Press.

Waterbury, John
1972   *North for the Trade: The Life and Times of a Berber Merchant.* Berkeley: University of California Press.

Watson, Lawrence C.
1976   Understanding a Life History as a Subjective Document: Hermeneutical and Phenomenological Perspectives. *Ethos* 4:95–131.

Westermarck, E.
1926   *Ritual and Belief in Morocco,* vols. 1 and 2. London: Macmillan.
1930   *Wit and Wisdom in Morocco: A Study of Native Proverbs.* London: George Routledge & Sons.

Zempleni, Andras
1977   From Symptom to Sacrifice: The Story of Khady Fall. Translated by Karen Merveille. Pp. 87–139 in V. Crapanzano and V. Garrison, eds., *Case Studies in Spirit Possession.* New York: John Wiley.

Index